HEALTHY LIVING

A Study of Colossians & Philemon

Melanie Newton

JOYFUL
WALK
BIBLE
STUDIES

We extend our heartfelt thanks to the many women who served as contributors to this study guide, especially our dear sister Joan Floyd who is now in heaven with Jesus. Without such wonderful help, we would never have accomplished this monumental task in a timely manner. Thanks also to the Thursday morning Bible class from RockPointe Church in Flower Mound whose insights helped me to make needed updates to the original study.

Healthy Living: Study of Colossians & Philemon

© 2025 Melanie Newton. All rights reserved.

Published by Joyful Walk Press. Flower Mound, TX

ISBN: 979-8-9925303-2-2

For questions about the use of this study guide or for bulk orders, please email us at melanienewton.com/contact.

Cover graphic adapted from "kaizen-valentines-day.jpg" graphic, a public domain online image.

Melanie Newton is the author of "Graceful Beginnings" books for anyone new to the Bible and "Joyful Walk Bible Studies" for established Christians. Her mission is to help women learn to study the Bible for themselves and to grow their Bible-teaching skills to lead others.

Joyful Walk Bible Studies are grace-based studies for women of all ages. Each study guide follows the inductive method of Bible study (observation, interpretation, application) in a warm and inviting format. We pray that you and your group will find *Healthy Living* a resource that God will use to strengthen you in your faith walk with Him.

Christ-Focused • *Grace-Based* • *Bible-Rich*

JOYFUL WALK PRESS
Flower Mound, TX

MELANIE NEWTON

Melanie Newton is a Louisiana girl who made the choice to follow Jesus while attending LSU. She and her husband Ron married and moved to Texas for him to attend Dallas Theological Seminary. They stayed in Texas where Ron led a wilderness camping ministry for troubled youth for many years. Ron now helps corporations with their challenging employees and is the author of the top-rated business book, *No Jerks on the Job*.

Melanie jumped into raising three Texas-born children and serving in ministry to women at her church. Through the years, the Lord has given her opportunity to do Bible teaching and to write grace-based Bible studies for women that are now available from her website (melanienewton.com) and on Bible.org. *Graceful Beginnings* books are for anyone new to the Bible. *Joyful Walk Bible Studies* are for maturing Christians.

Melanie Newton loves to help women learn how to study the Bible for themselves. She also teaches online courses for women to grow their Bible-teaching skills to help others—all with the goal of getting to know Jesus more along the way. Her heart's desire is to encourage you to have a joyful relationship with Jesus Christ so you are willing to share that experience with others around you.

Jesus took hold of me in 1972, and I've been on this great adventure ever since. My life is a gift of God, full of blessings in the midst of difficult challenges. The more I've learned and experienced God's absolutely amazing grace, the more I've discovered my faith walk to be a joyful one. I'm still seeking that joyful walk every day...

Melanie

OTHER BIBLE STUDIES BY MELANIE NEWTON

Graceful Beginnings Series books for anyone new to the Bible:

A Fresh Start (basics for new Christians)
Painting the Portrait of Jesus (the Gospel of John)
The God You Can Know (the character of God)
Grace Overflowing (an overview of Paul's 13 letters)
The Walk from Fear to Faith (7 Old Testament women)
Satisfied by His Love (women who knew Jesus)
Seek the Treasure (study of Ephesians)
Pathways to a Joyful Walk (6 pathways to a life filled with joy)

Joyful Walk Bible Studies for growing Christians:

Adorn Yourself with Godliness (1 Timothy and Titus, also in Spanish)
Everyday Women, Ever Faithful God (Old Testament women, also in Spanish)
Connecting Faith to Life on Planet Earth (Genesis 1-11; Revelation)
Graceful Living (the essentials for a grace-based Christian life)
Graceful Living Today (a devotional journal for a joyful life)
Healthy Living (Colossians and Philemon)
Heartbreak to Hope (the Gospel of Mark)
Identity: Sticking to Your Faith in a Pull-Apart World (Ezra thru Malachi)
Knowing Jesus, Knowing Joy (Philippians, also in Spanish)
Live Out His Love (New Testament women)
Perspective (1and 2 Thessalonians)
Profiles of Perseverance (Old Testament men, also in Spanish)
Radical Acts (Acts)
Reboot, Renew, Rejoice (1 and 2 Chronicles)
The God-Dependent Woman (2 Corinthians)
To Be Found Faithful (2 Timothy)

Resources for leading others

Be a Christ-Focused Small Group Leader
Leap into Lifestyle Disciplemaking
Bible Study Leadership Made Easy (online video course)
Painting the Picture of Jesus (the "I Am's" of Jesus lessons for children)
Teaching Children the God They Can Know (the character of God for children)

Download our catalogue and get resources for your spiritual growth at melanienewton.com.

Contents

Using This Study Guide

This study guide consists of 11 lessons covering two of Paul's letters—Colossians and Philemon. The lessons are divided into 5 sections (about 25 minutes in length). The first 4 sections contain a detail study of the passages. The fifth section is a podcast that provides additional insight to the lesson.

If you cannot do the entire lesson one week, please read the Bible passage covered by the lesson and try to do the "Day One Study" of the lesson.

THE BASIC STUDY

Each lesson includes core questions covering the passage narrative. These core questions will take you through the process of inductive Bible study—observation, interpretation, and application. The process is more easily understood in the context of answering these questions:

- What does the passage say? (Observation: what's actually there)

- What does it mean? (Interpretation: the author's intended meaning)

- How does this apply to me today? *(Application: making it personal)*

STUDY ENHANCEMENTS

Deeper Discoveries (optional): Embedded within the sections are *optional* questions for further research of subjects we don't have time to cover adequately in the lessons or contain information that may enhance the basic study. If you are meeting with a small group, your leader may give you the opportunity to share your "discoveries."

Study Aids: To aid in proper interpretation and application of the study, additional study aids are located where appropriate in the lesson:

- Historical Insights

- Scriptural Insight

- From the Greek (definitions of Greek words)

- Focus on the Meaning

- Think About It (thoughtful reflection)

Other useful study tools:

- **Blueletterbible.org** (or "Blue Letter Bible app) is especially helpful) to find cross references (verses with similar content to what you are studying) and meanings of the original Hebrew or Greek words or phrases used (usually called "interlinear"). You can also look at any verse in various Bible translations to help with understanding what it is saying.

- **Soniclight.com** is the website hosting *Dr. Tom Constable's Study Notes* on every book of the Bible, graciously provided by this much-loved professor at Dallas Theological Seminary. This is a great resource for additional research on any book we study— historical information, word meanings, scriptural insights, and discussion of difficult topics.

PODCASTS

Find podcasts for these lessons at melanienewton.com/podcasts (choose "3: Colossians) and on most podcast providers. Or you can read the blogs associated with the podcasts at melanienewton.com/blog. Choose Colossians category then scroll to find the title you want. Listen to the first podcast as an introduction to the study.

NEW TESTAMENT SUMMARY

The New Testament opens with the births of Jesus and John (known as "the baptist"). About 30 years later, John challenged the Jews to indicate their repentance (turning from sin and toward God) by submitting to water baptism—a familiar Old Testament practice used for repentance as well as when a Gentile converted to Judaism (to be washed clean of idolatry).

Jesus Christ, God's incarnate Son, publicly showed the world what God is like and taught His perfect ways for 3 – 3½ years. After preparing 12 disciples to continue Christ's earthly work, He died voluntarily on a cross for mankind's sin, rose from the dead, and returned to heaven. The account of His earthly life is recorded in 4 books known as the Gospels (the biblical books of Matthew, Mark, Luke and John named after the compiler of each account).

After Jesus' return to heaven, the followers of Christ were then empowered by the Holy Spirit and spread God's salvation message among the Jews, a number of whom believed in Christ. The apostle Paul and others traveling with him carried the good news to the Gentiles during 3 missionary journeys (much of this recorded in the book of Acts). Paul wrote 13 New Testament letters to churches & individuals (Romans through Philemon). The section in our Bible from Hebrews to Jude contains 8 additional letters penned by five men, including two apostles (Peter and John) and two of Jesus' half-brothers (James and Jude). The author of Hebrews is unknown. The apostle John also recorded Revelation, which summarizes God's final program for the world. The Bible ends as it began—with a new, sinless creation.

DISCUSSION GROUP GUIDELINES

Anyone can do this study alone. If you are doing this as part of a group, we suggest you use the following guidelines to maintain a safe environment for your group members to learn together.

1. **Attend consistently** whether your lesson is done or not. You'll learn from the other women, and they want to get to know you.

2. **Set aside time** to work through the study questions. The goal of Bible study is to **get to know** Jesus. He will change your life.

3. **Share your insights** from your personal study time. As you spend time in the Bible, Jesus will teach you truth through His Spirit inside you.

4. **Respect each other's insights**. Listen thoughtfully. Encourage each other as you interact. Refrain from dominating the discussion if you have a tendency to be talkative. ☺

5. **Celebrate our unity** in Christ. Avoid bringing up controversial subjects such as politics, divisive issues, and denominational differences.

6. **Maintain confidentiality.** Remember that anything shared during the group time is not to leave the **group** (unless permission is granted by the one sharing).

7. **Pray for one another** as sisters in Christ.

8. **Get to know the women** in your group. Please do not use your small group members for solicitation purposes for home businesses, though.

There is a small group discussion guide available at the end of this study. Anyone can use the guide to lead a group through a discussion of the questions in this study. This is especially useful for groups that have less than two hours to meet together.

Enjoy your Joyful Walk Bible Study!

Paul's Letter to the Colossians

New International Version (2011)

Paul, an apostle of Christ Jesus by the will of God, and Timothy our brother,

To God's holy people in Colossae, the faithful brothers and sisters in Christ:

Grace and peace to you from God our Father.

We always thank God, the Father of our Lord Jesus Christ, when we pray for you, because we have heard of your faith in Christ Jesus and of the love you have for all God's people— the faith and love that spring from the hope stored up for you in heaven and about which you have already heard in the true message of the gospel that has come to you. In the same way, the gospel is bearing fruit and growing throughout the whole world—just as it has been doing among you since the day you heard it and truly understood God's grace. You learned it from Epaphras, our dear fellow servant, who is a faithful minister of Christ on our behalf, and who also told us of your love in the Spirit.

For this reason, since the day we heard about you, we have not stopped praying for you. We continually ask God to fill you with the knowledge of His will through all the wisdom and understanding that the Spirit gives, so that you may live a life worthy of the Lord and please Him in every way: bearing fruit in every good work, growing in the knowledge of God, being strengthened with all power according to His glorious might so that you may have great endurance and patience, and giving joyful thanks to the Father, who has qualified you to share in the inheritance of His holy people in the kingdom of light. For He has rescued us from the dominion of darkness and brought us into the kingdom of the Son He loves, in whom we have redemption, the forgiveness of sins.

The Son is the image of the invisible God, the firstborn over all creation. For in Him all things were created: things in heaven and on earth, visible and invisible, whether thrones or powers or rulers or authorities; all things have been created through Him and for Him. He is before all things, and in Him all things hold together. And He is the head of the body, the church; He is the beginning and the firstborn from among the dead, so that in everything He might have the supremacy. For God was pleased to have all His fullness dwell in Him, and through Him to reconcile to Himself all things, whether things on earth or things in heaven, by making peace through His blood, shed on the cross.

Once you were alienated from God and were enemies in your minds because of your evil behavior. But now He has reconciled you by Christ's physical body through death to present you holy in His sight, without blemish and free from accusation— if you continue in your faith, established and firm, and do not move from the hope held out in the gospel. This is the gospel that you heard and that has been proclaimed to every creature under heaven, and of which I, Paul, have become a servant.

Now I rejoice in what I am suffering for you, and I fill up in my flesh what is still lacking in regard to Christ's afflictions, for the sake of His body, which is the church. I have become its servant by the commission God gave me to present to you the word of God in its fullness—the mystery that has been kept hidden for ages and generations, but is now disclosed to the Lord's people. To them God has chosen to make known among the Gentiles the glorious riches of this mystery, which is Christ in you, the hope of glory.

He is the one we proclaim, admonishing and teaching everyone with all wisdom, so that we may present everyone fully mature in Christ. To this end I strenuously contend with all the energy Christ so powerfully works in me.

I want you to know how hard I am contending for you and for those at Laodicea, and for all who have not met me personally. My goal is that they may be encouraged in heart and united in love, so that they may have the full riches of complete understanding, in order that they may know the mystery of God, namely, Christ, in whom are hidden all the treasures of wisdom and knowledge. I tell you this so that no one may deceive you by fine-sounding arguments. For though I am absent from you in body, I am present with you in spirit and delight to see how disciplined you are and how firm your faith in Christ is.

So then, just as you received Christ Jesus as Lord, continue to live your lives in Him, rooted and built up in Him, strengthened in the faith as you were taught, and overflowing with thankfulness.

See to it that no one takes you captive through hollow and deceptive philosophy, which depends on human tradition and the elemental spiritual forces of this world rather than on Christ.

For in Christ all the fullness of the Deity lives in bodily form, and in Christ you have been brought to fullness. He is the head over every power and authority. In Him you were also circumcised with a circumcision not performed by human hands. Your whole self ruled by the flesh was put off when you were circumcised by Christ, having been buried with Him in baptism, in which you were also raised with Him through your faith in the working of God, who raised Him from the dead.

When you were dead in your sins and in the uncircumcision of your flesh, God made you alive with Christ. He forgave us all our sins, having canceled the charge of our legal indebtedness, which stood against us and condemned us; He has taken it away, nailing it to the cross. And having disarmed the powers and authorities, He made a public spectacle of them, triumphing over them by the cross.

Therefore do not let anyone judge you by what you eat or drink, or with regard to a religious festival, a New Moon celebration or a Sabbath day. These are a shadow of the things that were to come; the reality, however, is found in Christ. Do not let anyone who delights in false humility and the worship of angels disqualify you. Such a person also goes into great detail about what they have seen; they are puffed up with idle notions by their unspiritual mind. They have lost connection with the head, from whom the whole body, supported and held together by its ligaments and sinews, grows as God causes it to grow.

Since you died with Christ to the elemental spiritual forces of this world, why, as though you still belonged to the world, do you submit to its rules: "Do not handle! Do not taste! Do not touch!"? These rules, which have to do with things that are all destined to perish with use, are based on merely human commands and teachings. Such regulations indeed have an appearance of wisdom, with their self-imposed worship, their false humility and their harsh treatment of the body, but they lack any value in restraining sensual indulgence.

Since, then, you have been raised with Christ, set your hearts on things above, where Christ is, seated at the right hand of God. Set your minds on things above, not on earthly things. For you died, and your life is now hidden with Christ in God. When Christ, who is your life, appears, then you also will appear with Him in glory.

Put to death, therefore, whatever belongs to your earthly nature: sexual immorality, impurity, lust, evil desires and greed, which is idolatry. Because of these, the wrath of God is coming. You used to walk in these ways, in the life you once lived. But now you must also rid yourselves of all such things as these: anger, rage, malice, slander, and filthy language from your lips. Do not lie to each other, since you have taken off your old self with its practices and have put on the new self, which is being renewed in knowledge in the image of its Creator. Here there is no Gentile or Jew, circumcised or uncircumcised, barbarian, Scythian, slave or free, but Christ is all, and is in all.

Therefore, as God's chosen people, holy and dearly loved, clothe yourselves with compassion, kindness, humility, gentleness and patience. Bear with each other and forgive one another if any of you has a grievance against someone. Forgive as the Lord forgave you. And over all these virtues put on love, which binds them all together in perfect unity.

Let the peace of Christ rule in your hearts, since as members of one body you were called to peace. And be thankful. Let the message of Christ dwell among you richly as you teach and admonish one another with all wisdom through psalms, hymns, and songs from the Spirit, singing to God with gratitude in your hearts. And whatever you do, whether in word or deed, do it all in the name of the Lord Jesus, giving thanks to God the Father through Him.

Wives, submit yourselves to your husbands, as is fitting in the Lord.

Husbands, love your wives and do not be harsh with them.

Children, obey your parents in everything, for this pleases the Lord.

Fathers, do not embitter your children, or they will become discouraged.

Slaves, obey your earthly masters in everything; and do it, not only when their eye is on you and to curry their favor, but with sincerity of heart and reverence for the Lord. Whatever you do, work at it with all your heart, as working for the Lord, not for human masters, since you know that you will receive an inheritance from the Lord as a reward. It is the Lord Christ you are serving. Anyone who does wrong will be repaid for their wrongs, and there is no favoritism.

Masters, provide your slaves with what is right and fair, because you know that you also have a Master in heaven.

Devote yourselves to prayer, being watchful and thankful. And pray for us, too, that God may open a door for our message, so that we may proclaim the mystery of Christ, for which I am in chains. Pray that I may proclaim it clearly, as I should. Be wise in the way you act toward outsiders; make the most of every opportunity. Let your conversation be always full of grace, seasoned with salt, so that you may know how to answer everyone.

Tychicus will tell you all the news about me. He is a dear brother, a faithful minister and fellow servant in the Lord. I am sending him to you for the express purpose that you may know about our circumstances and that he may encourage your hearts. He is coming with Onesimus, our faithful and dear brother, who is one of you. They will tell you everything that is happening here.

My fellow prisoner Aristarchus sends you his greetings, as does Mark, the cousin of Barnabas. (You have received instructions about him; if he comes to you, welcome him.) Jesus, who is called Justus, also sends greetings. These are the only Jews among my co-workers for the kingdom of God, and they have proved a comfort to me. Epaphras, who is one of you and a servant of Christ Jesus, sends greetings. He is always wrestling in prayer for you, that you may stand firm in all the will of God, mature and fully assured. I vouch for him that he is working hard for you and for those at Laodicea and Hierapolis. Our dear friend Luke, the doctor, and Demas send greetings. Give my greetings to the brothers and sisters at Laodicea, and to Nympha and the church in her house.

After this letter has been read to you, see that it is also read in the church of the Laodiceans and that you in turn read the letter from Laodicea.

Tell Archippus: "See to it that you complete the ministry you have received in the Lord."

I, Paul, write this greeting in my own hand. Remember my chains. Grace be with you.

Paul's Letter to Philemon

New International Version (2011)

Paul, a prisoner of Christ Jesus, and Timothy our brother,

To Philemon our dear friend and fellow worker—also to Apphia our sister and Archippus our fellow soldier—and to the church that meets in your home:

Grace and peace to you from God our Father and the Lord Jesus Christ.

I always thank my God as I remember you in my prayers, because I hear about your love for all His holy people and your faith in the Lord Jesus. I pray that your partnership with us in the faith may be effective in deepening your understanding of every good thing we share for the sake of Christ. Your love has given me great joy and encouragement, because you, brother, have refreshed the hearts of the Lord's people.

Therefore, although in Christ I could be bold and order you to do what you ought to do, yet I prefer to appeal to you on the basis of love. It is as none other than Paul—an old man and now also a prisoner of Christ Jesus—that I appeal to you for my son Onesimus, who became my son while I was in chains. Formerly he was useless to you, but now he has become useful both to you and to me.

I am sending him—who is my very heart—back to you. I would have liked to keep him with me so that he could take your place in helping me while I am in chains for the gospel. But I did not want to do anything without your consent, so that any favor you do would not seem forced but would be voluntary. Perhaps the reason he was separated from you for a little while was that you might have him back forever—no longer as a slave, but better than a slave, as a dear brother. He is very dear to me but even dearer to you, both as a fellow man and as a brother in the Lord.

So if you consider me a partner, welcome him as you would welcome me. If he has done you any wrong or owes you anything, charge it to me. I, Paul, am writing this with my own hand. I will pay it back—not to mention that you owe me your very self. I do wish, brother, that I may have some benefit from you in the Lord; refresh my heart in Christ. Confident of your obedience, I write to you, knowing that you will do even more than I ask.

And one thing more: Prepare a guest room for me, because I hope to be restored to you in answer to your prayers.

Epaphras, my fellow prisoner in Christ Jesus, sends you greetings. And so do Mark, Aristarchus, Demas and Luke, my fellow workers.

The grace of the Lord Jesus Christ be with your spirit.

> **Recommended:** Listen to the podcast "Truth Is the Prescription for Healthy Living" as an introduction to the whole study. Use the following listener guide.

Truth Is the Prescription for Healthy Living

Just as physical bodies are attacked by germs that make us sick, we are attacked by spiritual infections that leave us weak and dissatisfied. The only way to fight or avoid infection is to be satisfied by the truth of God we have in Jesus Christ. That gives us a strong immune system to fight and prevent spiritual infections.

WHAT IS A SPIRITUAL INFECTION?

- A spiritual infection=any opinion or belief that contradicts established biblical truth.

- The prescription for healthy living has three parts: 1) dwell in the truth of God you can know, 2) humbly accept what you don't know or understand, and 3) discern any teaching that you read or hear through the complete revelation of God's Word.

PRESCRIPTION PART 1: DWELL IN TRUTH YOU CAN KNOW.

- To dwell in truth is to make your home there. That means God's truth dominates your thoughts and attitudes, governs your life, and satisfies your heart.

- God gives us plenty of truth in the Bible that we can know and trust.

- God wants us to know the truth He has revealed to us, to make our home in that truth. *Ephesians 1:17-19*

PRESCRIPTION PART 2: HUMBLY ACCEPT WHAT YOU DON'T KNOW OR UNDERSTAND.

- Some things we read in the Bible we don't understand now but might in the future.

  "The secret things belong to the LORD our God, but the things revealed belong to us and to our children forever, that we may follow all the words of this law." (Deuteronomy 29:29)

- There is so much we can know now. But there are things we'll never know or understand.

- We must make the choice to humbly accept what we don't know or understand. And, be satisfied with it.

PRESCRIPTION PART 3: DISCERN ALL TEACHING THROUGH THE COMPLETE REVELATION OF GOD'S WORD.

Evaluate what you read and hear by comparing it with the whole Bible.

- Read any verse in the context of the passage where it is found—the paragraph, the chapter, and the book.

- Examine the original words to see what the writer meant and what the audience likely understood.

- Look at other verses with similar content to let the Bible interpret itself. And, you should always ask the Holy Spirit for understanding.

Avoid the "look-imagine-see" dragon when viewing any verse.

The "look-imagine-see" dragon shows up this way: someone *looks* at a verse or passage, *imagines* what they want it to say, then in their mind *sees* what they have imagined through twisting word meanings and interpretations. Once it starts, it's like a fiery dragon burning truth in its path. Cultural influence on Bible study feeds this dragon.

- Tame the "look-imagine-see dragon" by considering the Bible as sufficient on its own, not needing to be "improved."

- Tame the "look-imagine-see dragon" by basing your faith on what **is** in God's Word, not something you've just heard about it and not something you're imagining to be there.

- Tame the "look-imagine-see dragon" by following the inductive process for Bible Study—observation, interpretation, and application. Then, you can dwell in truth you can know.

> **Think About It:** We'll never know all there is to know about God. There will always be some mystery about Him. But there's enough revealed in the Bible to satisfy your desire to **know Him truthfully** and to know how to live your life in Christ truthfully.

Infection is bad. Untreated infection can be deadly. Knowing the truth of God that you have in Jesus Christ gives you an immune system that fights and prevents spiritual infection.

Let Jesus satisfy your heart needs with His truth and His love so you can get well and stay well.

1: The Gospel Received

Colossians 1:1-8

DAY ONE STUDY

The ABCs of Colossians and Philemon

AUTHOR

Paul identifies himself as the author of this letter written to the church at Colosse. Paul, whose Hebrew name was Saul, was born in Tarsus, a major Roman city on the coast of southeast Asia Minor. Tarsus was the center for the tent making industry; Paul was trained in that craft as his occupation (his primary paying profession). As a Jewish Pharisee from the tribe of Benjamin, Paul was trained at the feet of Gamaliel, a well-respected rabbi of the day. Saul was an ardent persecutor of the early church until his life changing conversion to Christianity.

After believing in Jesus Christ as his Savior, Paul was called by God to take the gospel to the Gentiles. This was an amazing about-face for a committed Pharisee like Paul who ordinarily would have nothing to do with Gentiles. Paul wrote 13 letters that are included in the New Testament. Tradition has it that Paul was beheaded shortly after he wrote 2nd Timothy in 67 AD.

BACKGROUND

The country village of Colosse lay in the beautiful Lycus Valley about 100 miles east of Ephesus in modern Turkey. It was 1 of 3 ancient towns (Colosse, Hierapolis, and Laodicea) situated close to each other along a major trade route between the big city of Ephesus to the west and the Euphrates River to the east. What each city did affected the others. The population of Colosse was mostly Gentile of Greek descent. But a large Jewish group had been relocated there from Mesopotamia by Antiochus in the second century BC, bringing with them eastern influences. Because of being near a major trade route, the town was influenced by ideas and practices from both the east (Mesopotamia) and the west (Rome). So, the mindset was mainly Greek with influx of new ideas from the East and other parts of the Roman Empire. Over time, the road system changed, and Colosse lost its importance. Laodicea became the greater city. In the 7th-8th centuries, the people moved to a fortress south of the city and in the 12th century, the Turks destroyed Colosse. Today, Colosse is composed of uninhabited ruins. Motorist guides to Turkey point out Laodicea's ruins but do not even mention Colosse.

On his third missionary journey, Paul spent 3 years in Ephesus (~54-57 A.D), a large city of 250,000 people. While there, Paul held classes every day for anyone wanting to learn about Jesus Christ, having their sins forgiven, and gaining a new way to live. The gospel spread throughout that part of Asia Minor. One of Paul's students named Epaphras traveled 100 miles east back to his hometown of Colosse to bring the gospel to the people living there. A few Jews believed the message about Jesus, but it was mostly the Greeks and Romans who listened and trusted in Jesus to take away their sins. They started worshiping God together as a church. Epaphras also started churches in Hierapolis and Laodicea. The churches grew larger. Then, false teaching began to infiltrate them.

While Paul was imprisoned in Rome for 2 years, Epaphras headed to Rome to discuss with Paul what was happening back home. The church was now about 5 years old. Paul had never met the Colossians, but he loved these young Christians very much. The heresy (an opinion or belief that contradicts established religious truth) that Paul discovered in Colosse was like an infection in the Body of Christ there. False teachers taught that Jesus was not *the* Lord, just *a* lord. They were teaching that faith in Jesus was not enough for them to be spiritual. They needed to add other "experiences" to the mix. To contradict this infection, we find in Colossians the greatest declaration of Christ's deity and sufficiency found in Scripture.

> **Focus on the Meaning:** I love this truthful phrase regarding Jesus Christ and our salvation through Him that was so aptly worded by a dear Bible teacher in the 1980's (Vickie Kraft). *"Jesus Christ is above all powers and authorities, in all believers, and is all we need for earth and heaven!"* 'Nuff said. We are going to hang onto that truth!

Context

From his prison confinement, Paul wrote a general letter to pass around to the whole region of Asia Minor (the letter to the Ephesians) as well as a letter specifically to the churches in the Colossian area (the letter we know as Colossians). He wrote a third letter, a personal one, to a rich landowner named Philemon about his runaway slave Onesimus. These three letters plus the one to the Philippians are called the "Prison Epistles" since Paul wrote them while he was imprisoned in Rome. Paul's co-worker Tychicus delivered the letters to Ephesus and Colosse. Onesimus delivered the personal letter to his master, Philemon.

Colossians is found in the New Testament with Ephesians and Philippians, the other two letters written about the same time during Paul's first imprisonment in Rome. Philemon, though written at the same time as Colossians, is the shortest and so is located at the end of the letters from Paul. As you will discover, small doesn't mean less important.

1. What grabbed your attention from the ABCs above?

Healthy Living

Every parent knows that when a baby is burning with fever, there's an infection in the small child's body! You know how to recognize an infection in a physical body by its symptoms.

The same is true regarding a spiritual infection. Any opinion or belief that contradicts established biblical truth can cause an infection in the Body of Christ. The term used to describe that is "heresy." It's not just error; it is anti-truth! And like an infection in the human body, heresy always affects life so it must be addressed.

A spiritual infection is usually fed by looking to the wrong places to get your heart needs satisfied. The results are disappointment, fear, resentment, and many other negative thoughts and behaviors.

Thankfully, the answer to all spiritual infections is the truth that has been given to us in the Bible, especially in the New Testament. Knowing truth gives us a spiritual immune system that fights and prevents infection in our hearts and minds. Truth is the prescription for healthy living.

This prescription for healthy living has three parts: First, you dwell in the truth of God you can know. Next, you humbly accept what you don't know or understand. And then, you discern any teaching that you read or hear through the complete revelation of God's Word. These three parts help you to fight spiritual infections or prevent their influence over you.

We will see how that works throughout this study of Colossians and Philemon. We'll never know all there is to know about God. There will always be some mystery about Him. But there's enough revealed in the Bible to satisfy your desire to **know him truthfully** and to know how to live your life in Christ truthfully.

Infection is bad. Untreated infection can be deadly. Knowing the truth of God that you have in Jesus Christ gives you an immune system that fights and prevents spiritual infection. Let Jesus satisfy your heart needs with His truth and His love so you can get well and stay well.

2. Have you recognized an area of your life where you have been infected by some kind of teaching that contradicts established biblical truth?

Respond to the Lord about what He has shown you today.

Day Two Study: Get the Big Picture of Colossians

Ask the Lord Jesus to teach you through His Word.

In all of our *Joyful Walk Bible Studies*, we follow the inductive process for Bible Study. The inductive process starts with observation, looking carefully at what the text actually says. *What does the Bible say?* The next step is interpretation, which is trying to understand the author's intended meaning—to him and to the audience who would read or hear it. *What does it mean?* Once you know what the Bible says and what it means, then you are ready for application, which is learning how to live this out in your life. *What application will you make?* When you follow the inductive process for Bible Study, you will be able to confidently dwell in that truth.

What does the Bible say? (This is the "Observation" step in the process of Bible Study.)

Where do we begin? Have you ever heard the saying, "You can't see the forest for the trees?" The best way to study any book of the Bible is to begin with the "forest" (survey the whole) and then proceed to the "trees" (the individual parts). We will start by getting an overview of what Paul wrote in his letter to the Colossians.

Today, read the letter called Colossians at one sitting. Read it as it was intended—a letter from one dear friend to another. It will take about 8 minutes. You can read the letter in any translation of the Bible you choose. A copy of Colossians (NIV translation) is included in this study guide before Lesson One. Feel free to mark anything that grabs your attention and look for the main topics. Then, answer the questions below. Ready? Go!

3. What grabbed your attention from this first reading of Paul's letter?

4. What would you say were the main subjects that Paul covered in this letter?

5. What issues seem to be bothering the Colossian church?

6. Skim over the letter again. Using the letter printed in this study guide before Lesson One:

   - Mark anything that refers to being "in Christ" (also in Him, by Him, through Him, with Him, in the Lord).

     How many times does Paul emphasize this relationship? _____

   - Paul, the master communicator, often uses the enemy's very own words to refute bad teaching. Mark "fullness," "complete," "mystery," "knowledge," and "wisdom" (plus any variations on these words).

     How many times does he use these terms? _____

7. What questions do you have after reading Colossians that you hope to be answered in this study?

Think About It: The whole book deals with the difference between being captured by a world that sucks the life out of you versus willingly binding yourself to the life-giving Lord Jesus. (Wayne Braudrick, Frisco Bible Church sermon "Faithful," 6/7/2015)

Respond to the Lord about what you learned today. Ask God to show you what He wants you to learn through this study of Colossians.

Day Three Study

What does the Bible say? *(This is the "Observation" step in the process of Bible Study.)*

Ask the Lord Jesus to teach you through His Word.

Let's start digging into this wonderful letter from God to us. For every lesson, we will begin with reading the whole passage to get the big picture before we study the verses more closely.

Read the Bible passage below (NIV). Use your own method (colored pencils, lines, shapes) to mark 1) anything that grabs your attention, 2) words you want to understand, and 3) topics you have seen before in this letter. Draw arrows between thoughts that connect.

1 *Paul, an apostle of Christ Jesus by the will of God, and Timothy our brother,*

2 To God's holy people in Colossae, the faithful brothers and sisters in Christ: Grace and peace to you from God our Father.

3 We always thank God, the Father of our Lord Jesus Christ, when we pray for you, 4 because we have heard of your faith in Christ Jesus and of the love you have for all God's people— 5 the faith and love that spring from the hope stored up for you in heaven and about which you have already heard in the true message of the gospel 6 that has come to you. In the same way, the gospel is bearing fruit and growing throughout the whole world—just as it has been doing among you since the day you heard it and truly understood God's grace. 7 You learned it from Epaphras, our dear fellow servant, who is a faithful minister of Christ on our behalf, 8 and who also told us of your love in the Spirit.

8. As you read any of Paul's letters, be sure to pay attention to the introductions. What important information does Paul include in the first two verses of his letter to the Colossians?

    • Verse 1—

    • Verse 2—

    From the Greek: Whereas older translations used the all-inclusive word "brothers" in verse 2, the Greek word (*adelphoi*) refers here to believers, both men and women, as part of God's family. The NIV translators have chosen "brothers and sisters" to use here for clarity. You will also see this in Colossians 4:15.

9. Look at the first 3-4 verses of Paul's other letters (start with Romans then go through Philemon.) In how many of them does He refer to Jesus as "Lord Jesus Christ?" Note: "Lord" (Gr. *kyrios*) means "master, sovereign." Does Paul consistently teach the same thing about Jesus to all the churches or just to the Colossians?

What does it mean? *(This is the "Interpretation" step in the process of Bible Study.)*

Paul starts with a conversational, inspiring tone as he moves toward establishing truth and combatting error.

10. Looking at vv. 3-8:

- What did Paul say about their faith, love and hope (vv. 3-5)?

> **From the Greek:** The phrase "true message of the gospel" translates two Greek words: *evangelion* (the term Jesus made up for the good news of the gospel) and *aletheia* (historically factual, valid, can always be counted on). Together, they translate as "gospel truth." This is the first use in literature of this now-common phrase referring to God's truth found in the gospel.

- What else about this church made Paul excited and thankful (vv. 6-8)?

> **Scriptural Insight:** The Holy Spirit had created love for Paul in the Colossians. This is the only reference to the Holy Spirit in this epistle. In Colossians Paul ascribed the activities of God that he normally associated with the Holy Spirit to Christ. He probably did this to glorify Jesus Christ before the Colossians who were being taught that Christ was less than He is. (*Dr. Constable's Notes on Colossians 2020 Edition,* p. 17)

11. ***Deeper Discoveries (optional):*** Look up these passages to discover how the three words faith, hope and love are related to one another and are manifested in a believer's life— Galatians 5:5-6; 1 Thessalonians 1:2-3, 5:8; Hebrews 10:22-24 and 1 Peter 1:3-5, 22.

12. Since Paul had not met these people, how do we know the Colossians had received the complete gospel from Epaphras?

13. Read Acts 2:22-24; 16:30-31; and 1 Corinthians 15:3-4. From the very beginning, what was taught as the gospel truth?

14. What is the significance of Paul stressing that the gospel they received had been bearing fruit everywhere?

Think About It: Heresies (such as the one at Colosse) are local and harmful; but truth is universal and helpful. One of the unmistakable characteristics of the true gospel is God's grace in all its truth. Some preach a "different gospel—which is really no gospel at all" (Gal. 1:6-7). This is because it is a gospel of grace plus works, or faith plus works. But the true gospel is one of grace alone (Romans 11:6; Ephesians 2:8-9; Titus 3:5-7). (*The Bible Knowledge Commentary New Testament,* p. 670)

Gospel truth declares that our salvation is by grace alone through faith alone in Christ alone.

What application will you make for healthy living? (This is the "Application" step in the process of Bible Study.)

15. When did you hear the gospel and trust its message? Did what you receive match what Paul and Epaphras preached?

Respond to the Lord about what He has shown you today.

DAY FOUR STUDY: TRUTH—THE PRESCRIPTION FOR HEALTHY LIVING

Ask the Lord Jesus to teach you through His Word.

Heresy (an opinion or belief that contradicts established religious TRUTH) is an infection in the Body of Christ. Heresy is not just error; it's anti-truth! And like an infection in the human body, heresy always affects one's spiritual health (as well as emotional, mental, and sometimes physical health). So, heresy must be addressed. It cannot be ignored. Thankfully, the answer to all heresy is TRUTH! Knowing truth gives us a spiritual immune system that fights and prevents infection. That is the prescription for healthy living. Here's how it works:

Dwell in Truth You Can Know

To "dwell" means to make your home in. It's what dominates your thoughts and attitudes, governs your life, and has the most influence on you. God gives us plenty of truth in the Scriptures that we can know and trust. There are 66 books of revelation given. 1189 chapters. If we just took 1 chapter per day and wrote down all the truths about God and our relationship with Him that is revealed to us, it would take us more than 3 years to get through the whole Bible! God wants us to know the truth He has revealed. He wants us to make our home— to dwell— in that truth. It is for our own good!

16. Read Ephesians 1:17-19. List all the truths Paul said we could know about our God.

17. Reread Colossians 1:1-8. List the truths about God and His relationship to us that we can KNOW.

Look at all that God says we can KNOW! Each passage we read or study has plenty of truth that we can KNOW with certainty and allow to govern our lives. DWELL in truth you can know.

Humbly Accept the "I Don't Know or Understand"

In the midst of all 1189 chapters in the Bible are verses we just don't understand. Perhaps you don't understand it now but will in the future as you get more confident in Bible study and hear great teaching that helps you understand. But there are things we will never know or understand.

18. Read Deuteronomy 29:29. What does it declare?

Notice the emphasis on the things revealed— we can KNOW them. But there are "secret things" the Lord has not revealed yet. As we study the Bible, we can do our best to try to understand what is written—examining the original words to see what the writer meant and what the audience understood, looking at cross-references to let the Bible interpret itself, and asking the Spirit for understanding. But you may never understand something you read. Don't let that unnerve you.

19. Make note of anything in Colossians 1:1-8 that you do not understand at this time.

DWELL in truth you can know (the list you made in Question 17). And, HUMBLY ACCEPT the "I don't know or understand."

Discern Teaching through the Complete Revelation of God's Word

To dwell in the truth of God's Word, we must **discern what we read and hear** by comparing it with the complete revelation of God's Word. We can't extract pieces of it and build our foundation on that. Nor should we build our faith on experiences and feelings. There's junk out there about God so it's important to really get to know the God of the Bible.

Avoid the "look-imagine-see" way of looking at any verse, which leads to error. What do I mean by "look-imagine-see?" Someone *looks* at a verse or passage, *imagines* what they want it to say, and then *"sees"* in their mind what they have imagined through twisting word meanings and interpretations.

Cultural influence on Bible study feeds this "look-imagine-see" process. You look at the passage, imagine a way for it to fit a particular cultural slant, then you see what you want to see. Many types of false teaching through the years have started with this kind of "look-imagine-see" process. Avoid doing that by following the inductive process of Bible Study: observation (what the text says), interpretation (what was the author's intended meaning—to him and to his audience that would read or hear it), and application (how to live this out in your life). That is the best way to study the Bible. Look at what's there. Learn what it means and teaches you. Then, live it out in your life.

You want to make sure you are basing your faith on what is in God's Word, not something you have heard before and not something you are imagining to be there. So, avoid that "look-imagine-see" way of looking at the Bible.

We will never know all there is to know about God. There'll always be some mystery about Him. But there's enough revealed in the Bible that we can KNOW HIM TRUTHFULLY and know how to live our life in Christ truthfully. The Holy Spirit uses the Scripture we read and study to teach us about our God so we can know TRUTH and DWELL in that truth.

20. Every week, we will ask you to evaluate something you have read or heard in light of the TRUTH you are learning—books, social media, billboards—things that sound nice and comfy but may actually lead to or be based upon error in biblical thinking. I may even throw one into the lesson for you to evaluate and discern truth or error. Does anything come to mind that fits with today's lesson? Use specific verses to discern truth from error in any saying or teaching.

Respond to the Lord about what He has shown you today.

Recommended: Listen to the podcast "Escape the Cultural Captivity Infection" to reinforce what you have learned. Use the following listener guide.

Escape the Cultural Captivity Infection

In the last podcast, I told you that any opinion or belief that contradicts established biblical truth can cause an infection in a Christian's heart and mind. It's usually not just error, but anti-truth. Such a spiritual infection always affects life so it must be addressed. A spiritual infection is usually fed by looking to the wrong places to get your heart needs satisfied. The results are disappointment, fear, resentment, and many other negative thoughts and behaviors.

Thankfully, the answer to all spiritual infections is the truth that has been given to us in the Bible, especially in the New Testament. Knowing truth gives us a spiritual immune system that fights and prevents infection in our hearts and minds. Truth is the prescription for healthy living.

The first step, though, is recognizing the infection.

DR. PAUL DIAGNOSED INFECTION IN COLOSSE.

Paul knew that the Colossians had received the complete gospel from Epaphras. They got God's grace in all its truth. And it was powerful enough to meet their every spiritual need. So, what happened?

> *See to it that no one takes you captive through hollow and deceptive philosophy, which depends on human tradition and the elemental spiritual forces of this world rather than on Christ. (Colossians 2:8)*

WHAT IS THE CULTURAL CAPTIVITY INFECTION?

You've seen enough movies to be able to picture in your mind what it would look like to be taken captive. Some of you've been in bondage to something that has taken you captive. You understand that.

- Paul said hollow and deceptive philosophy had taken them captive.

- Human philosophies that do not worship Christ are under the influence of Satan and his demons.

- Before Christ, we were subject to those "spiritual forces." Through union with Christ, we die to them and are no longer bound to obey them.

- When considering anyone's philosophy, the qualifying test is this: **Where does Jesus fit into their thinking and philosophy**—as *a* way to know God or *the* way to know God?

WHAT MAKES US SUSCEPTIBLE TO THIS CULTURAL CAPTIVITY INFECTION?

> "Cultural captivity looks to the culture rather than to Christ and the Bible as truth and a primary guide for living. Cultural captivity is usually caused by 3 things: Putting our trust in something other than the person or promises of Christ. Misunderstanding the truths by which Christ has called us to live. Or, a combination of both." (Probe Ministries, probe.org)

The Colossian church had been infected with philosophy from their culture. There were three main symptoms of this infection:

- Symptom #1: Dethroning Jesus Christ.

- Symptom #2: Emphasizing works.

- Symptom #3: Elevating experiences.

TRUTH IS THE PRESCRIPTION FOR CULTURAL CAPTIVITY

In Colossians, Paul writes the strongest statement of the supremacy and deity of Christ found anywhere in the New Testament. The Greek words he used are specific for this infection, just like a doctor's prescription to treat a specific disease. There was no way those reading or listening to this letter could possibly misunderstand anything that Paul was telling them. The truth about Jesus would satisfy their heart needs. They wouldn't need to look anywhere else.

As you study Colossians, you may discover that you have a concept about Jesus Christ, salvation, or the Christian life that is based on human tradition or philosophy instead of on Scripture.

Do you have the Cultural Captivity infection regarding who Jesus Christ is? For healthy living, you will need to recognize that infection and give it up to accept the truth about Christ presented in God's Word.

Infection is bad. Untreated infection can be deadly. Knowing the truth of God that you have in Jesus Christ gives you an immune system that fights and prevents spiritual infection.

Let Jesus satisfy your heart needs with His truth and His love so you can get well and stay well.

2: A Life Worthy

Colossians 1:9-14

DAY ONE STUDY—GET THE BIG PICTURE

Ask the Lord Jesus to teach you through His Word.

What does the Bible say?

Read the Bible passage below (NIV) including verses from the last lesson. Use your own method (colored pencils, lines, shapes) to mark 1) anything that grabs your attention, 2) words you want to understand, and 3) topics you have seen before in this letter. Draw arrows between thoughts that connect.

1 *Paul, an apostle of Christ Jesus by the will of God, and Timothy our brother,*

² To God's holy people in Colossae, the faithful brothers and sisters in Christ: Grace and peace to you from God our Father.

³ We always thank God, the Father of our Lord Jesus Christ, when we pray for you, ⁴ because we have heard of your faith in Christ Jesus and of the love you have for all God's people— ⁵ the faith and love that spring from the hope stored up for you in heaven and about which you have already heard in the true message of the gospel ⁶ that has come to you. In the same way, the gospel is bearing fruit and growing throughout the whole world—just as it has been doing among you since the day you heard it and truly understood God's grace. ⁷ You learned it from Epaphras, our dear fellow servant, who is a faithful minister of Christ on our behalf, ⁸ and who also told us of your love in the Spirit.

⁹ For this reason, since the day we heard about you, we have not stopped praying for you. We continually ask God to fill you with the knowledge of his will through all the wisdom and understanding that the Spirit gives, ¹⁰ so that you may live a life worthy of the Lord and please him in every way: bearing fruit in every good work, growing in the knowledge of God, ¹¹ being strengthened with all power according to his glorious might so that you may have great endurance and patience, ¹² and giving joyful thanks to the Father, who has qualified you to share in the inheritance of his holy people in the kingdom of light. ¹³ For he has rescued us from the dominion of darkness and brought us into the kingdom of the Son he loves, ¹⁴ in whom we have redemption, the forgiveness of sins.

1. What grabbed your attention from verses 9-14?

2. What specific words or phrases do you want to understand better?

3. What words or phrases are repeated in verses 9-14? Give verses.

4. What topics (if any) in verses 9-14 have we studied in previous lessons? Give verses.

5. *Healthy Living:* From this lesson's passage (1:9-14), choose one verse to dwell upon all week long. Write it in the space below. Ask God to teach you through this verse.

Respond to the Lord about what you learned today.

DAY TWO STUDY

Read Colossians 1:1-14. Ask the Lord Jesus to teach you through His Word.

What does it mean?

6. Focus on v. 9. Using any dictionary (regular or Bible dictionary), define these words:

    *   Knowledge—

    *   Wisdom—

    *   Understanding—

Summary: What did Paul ask God to do?

> **Focus on the Meaning:** Paul used two key words, "fill" and "knowledge." The first suggest a filling out to completeness, and the latter suggests a full, deep understanding. Such knowledge of God's will does not come from a fleshly mind (which "puffs up," 1 Cor. 8:1), but from the Holy Spirit who enlightens a believer's inner person (1 Cor. 2:5-6, 13), and from the Word of God. God's will, revealed in the Bible, is made known to believers by the Holy Spirit's teaching ministry. (*The Bible Knowledge Commentary New Testament,* p. 670)

7. Paul mentions the knowledge of God's revealed will and includes 4 specific areas included in His will for us as believers.

> **Focus on the Meaning:** The "will" (*thelematos*) of God is what God has revealed in His Word to be correct, regarding both belief (faith) and behavior (works, morality; cf. Colossians 4:12; Acts 22:14; Romans 12:2). (*Dr. Constable's Notes on Colossians 2020 Edition,* p. 19)

- God wants you to know His will so that we can do what (beginning of verse 10)?

- Why should you want to do this?

> **Think About It:** The aim of believers in all their worthy conduct should be to please Him in every way, to anticipate and do His wishes in every aspect of life (cf. Eph. 5:10). (*The Bible Knowledge Commentary New Testament,* p. 671)

What application will you make for healthy living?

8. Using Paul's prayer in Colossians 1:9-12, pray for specific people you know. Look for evidence of God working in their lives according to His Word in this passage.

Respond to the Lord about what He has shown you today.

DAY THREE STUDY

Read Colossians 1:9-14. Ask the Lord Jesus to teach you through His Word.

What does it mean?

9. Paul's prayer for these believers includes the *evidence* of a life worthy and pleasing to God (and His will for us!) in four specific areas. Fill in the chart below.

Evidence of a life worthy & pleasing to God	How that would look in someone's life
1. bearing…	
2. growing…	
3. being…	
4. giving…	

> **From the Greek:** In verse 10, "strengthened" means enabled. "Power" means the ability to exert force especially in a non-physical sense. "Might" means power to direct, the capacity to be in charge. The Triune God empowers humans who trust Jesus. That power comes from the One who is in charge, and it allows us to be powerful in the non-physical battles of life. (Wayne Braudrick, Frisco Bible Church sermon "Powerful," 6/14/2015)

10. According to verse 11, who gives you the ability to live a life worthy of the Lord and pleasing to Him?

Can you do this through your own efforts? Why not?

Think About It: Human parents raise their children to become more independent of them over time. God raises His children to become more dependent on Him over time. Dependent living is recognizing you can do nothing worthy of pleasing God on your own efforts. Dependent living is learning to say to Jesus, "Lord, I can't do this on my own. But you can in and through me. I will trust you." Then, watch what He does.

11. In verse 12, Paul says, "who has qualified you (made you competent) to share in the inheritance of the saints." How did God qualify us? Dig into all of Chapter 1 for this answer!! Add any other verses you already know as well.

Focus on the Meaning: God has qualified you (lit. "made you competent;" cf. 2 Cor. 3:6) to share in the inheritance of the saints...though believers are unfit in themselves, God has fitted them. (*The Bible Knowledge Commentary New Testament,* p. 671-672)

12. ***Deeper Discoveries (optional):*** Read these other prayers of Paul—Ephesians 1:17-19; Ephesians 3:16-19 and Philippians 1:9-11. Why is it beneficial to use these words to pray for your saved loved ones? For those unsaved, pray for them to accept the good news gift.

13. "Dominion" in v. 13 means "tyranny/ rule." Read Ephesians 2:1-3 and 2 Corinthians 4:4. Before trusting in Christ, what was our experience in the dominion of darkness (in which we are born as sinners)?

Scriptural Insight: Satan is not the direct cause of sin in humans. However, he rules the fallen world; the unsaved are part of his domain. He is now doing all in his power to keep the unsaved from being delivered from his dominion of darkness and transferred into Christ's kingdom of light. He energizes the children of disobedience (Ephesians 2:2) and blinds the minds of the unsaved so the light of the gospel can't reach them (2 Corinthians 4:4).

14. How do we get into Christ's kingdom (v. 13)?

Historical Insight: The verb translated "transferred" (*metestesen*) described the relocation of large groups of people such as captured armies or colonists from one country to another. This kingdom is probably a reference to Christ's domain as opposed to Satan's domain of darkness..."Darkness" is also a prominent figure in biblical symbolism where it represents ignorance, falsehood, and sin. (*Dr. Constable's Notes on Colossians 2020 Edition,* pp. 22-23

15. What do we receive there (v. 14)?

16. What is redemption, and how is it related to forgiveness? Use a dictionary or Bible dictionary to derive your answer.

What application will you make for healthy living?

17. *Pleasing God with your life:*

- Is it your desire to live a life worthy and pleasing to God? Why?

- Which of those 4 evidences of a life worthy and pleasing to God in vv. 10-12 will you trust God's power to do in your life today?

18. *Respond to the Lord about what He has shown you today.* Meditate on and then respond to what it means to be transferred from the dominion of darkness to the kingdom of the Son of God. Feel free to use any creative means (poem, prose, song, drawing, art).

DAY FOUR STUDY: TRUTH—THE PRESCRIPTION FOR HEALTHY LIVING

Ask the Lord Jesus to teach you through His Word.

Dwell in Truth You Can Know

19. Review the Colossians passage we studied in this lesson. List the truths about God and His relationship to us that we can KNOW.

Humbly Accept the "I Don't Know or Understand"

20. Make note of anything in the Colossians passage we studied in this lesson that you do not understand at this time.

Discern Teaching through the Complete Revelation of God's Word

21. To evaluate something you read or hear in light of the TRUTH you are learning—books, social media, billboards—things that sound nice and comfortable but may actually lead to or be based upon error in biblical thinking, use the following suggested process.

   • Step #1: Define the terms and issues involved.

   • Step #2: Ask questions and support your answers with Scripture, looking for truth you can know and what you can't know.

   • Step #3: Think of a graceful response to someone holding to that type of thinking.

Here's an example:

After her beloved Christian mother died, a grieving woman needed comfort. To help with her grief, she drew from something she had heard in the culture—that her mother had now become an angel and was present with her, communicating with her. So, let's work through the process of discerning truth from error and responding graciously.

Step #1: Define the issues/terms.

There are really three issues involved: 1. Do Christians become angels when they die? 2. Can our loved ones in heaven see what is happening in our lives on earth and communicate with us? 3. When grieving, how do we turn to Jesus for our comfort rather than traditions that make us feel good but draw us away from Him?

Step #2: Ask questions and support your answers with Scripture, looking for truth you can know and what you can't know.

Continuing with the example given:

1. Do Christians become angels when they die? The biblical truth is that angels and people are clearly distinct in their creation, purpose and destiny (Colossians 1:15-17; Hebrews 1:13-14). People do not become angels when they die. Our greatest confirmation of this is Jesus Himself. After His resurrection, He appeared in a human body, the same kind we will receive after we die. We will be like Him (Philippians 3:20-21; 1 John 3:2). **Here's the truth we can know: people become like Christ when they die, not like angels.**

2. Can our loved ones in heaven see what is happening in our lives on earth and communicate with us? The Bible doesn't clearly tell us if people in heaven are able to observe what happens on earth. The witnesses of Hebrews 12:1 are those Old Testament believers who can testify that it is possible to live a life of faith because they did it. The text doesn't say they are watching us. And, that would not include anyone who died since the Old Testament ended anyway. Can people in heaven communicate with us? The Bible teaches that people on earth are not to communicate with the dead (Deuteronomy 18:10-12). Loved ones in heaven are without sin and will not disobey God so they will not try to communicate with us. Feathers, pennies, etc. are normal events and can serve as reminders for us of our loved ones but are not communications from them. **Here's the "I don't know" we must humbly accept: we cannot know if our dead loved ones see anything happening on earth.** That is a secret thing belonging to the Lord (Deuteronomy 29:29). Anything else is speculation.

3. When grieving, how do we turn to Jesus for our comfort rather than traditions that make us feel good but draw us away from Him? Our God promises to be a God of comfort and fulfills that promise (2 Corinthians 1:3-5). We should turn to Jesus first for our comfort and let Him choose how He does that for us. He uses people who give us hugs, listen to us talk about our loved one, cry with us, and help us when we are weak. Memories of our loved ones are stimulated by sounds, places, sights, smells, and many other reminders associated with that person in our lives. We can take comfort from those stimulated memories and thank God for them. The Holy Spirit pours out Jesus' love in our hearts (Romans 5:5) so we can inwardly feel loved by Him during those times of grief. Jesus can also use His angels who are servants of God as ministering spirits to us (Hebrews 1:14). God's angels (not people angels) are present around us and can influence things happening so as to minister to us. If you feel your loved one close to you, it is likely an angel Jesus has sent to be near you at that time. **Here's the truth: Jesus uses people, memories, His Spirit, His love, and His angels to comfort us in a time of grief.**

Step #3: Think of a graceful response to someone holding to that type of thinking.

Continuing with the example given:

I feel how much you are hurting since your mother's death and how much you miss her. While you loved your mom so much that thinking of her as an angel gives you comfort, the Bible teaches this truth that God is giving her a wonderful resurrected human body like Jesus has, not an angel's body. You have wonderful memories of your mom that will crop up through places, smells, sights, and other reminders of your life with her. And, Jesus will comfort you in your grief through those memories, through people He sends to cry with you and help you, through His Spirit pouring love into your heart, and through true angels who will be near you to minister to you in amazing ways during this sad time. Stay focused on the comfort you will receive from Jesus and let your heart just be completely hugged by Him.

Your turn:

Using the process suggested above, how would you evaluate this one and prepare a gracious response to a believer who thinks this is biblical:

"Do your best and let God do the rest."

Respond to the Lord about what He has shown you today.

Recommended: Listen to the podcast "Resist the Tyranny of the Urgent Infection" to reinforce what you have learned. Use the following listener guide.

Resist the "Tyranny of the Urgent" Infection

In Colossians 1:9-14, Paul asks God to fill the Colossian Christians with knowledge and understanding about His will so that they would live a life worthy of the Lord Jesus. The prayer is that they would know the Lord so well that they will gain wisdom for their daily lives. From this wisdom, they would apply what they know to various situations they face through clear analysis and decision-making. The result is living a life that pleases the Lord Jesus in every way.

THE TYRANNY OF THE URGENT INFECTION

"We live in a constant tension between the urgent and the important. ... Often urgent, though less important, tasks call for immediate response. ... The appeal of these demands seems irresistible, and they devour our energy. But in the light of eternity, their momentary prominence fades. With a sense of loss, we recall the important tasks that have been [set] aside. We realize that we've become slaves to the tyranny of the urgent." (Charles E. Hummel, *Tyranny of the Urgent*)

- Sometimes, the urgent is also the important. That's not the "Tyranny of the Urgent" infection.

- In our extreme busyness answering those endless urgent demands, we often can't see which ones are truly important any longer. Because we do it to ourselves, it's really an intentional blindness.

"Intentional blindness is the trick our own brains play on us—keeping us preoccupied with one thing while leaving us unaware and oblivious to another." (Priscilla Shirer)

WHAT MAKES US SUSCEPTIBLE TO THIS INFECTION?

- For many of us, it's the desire to satisfy others' expectations of us.

- When we don't stop to evaluate how we're spending our time, we can become blinded by the poisonous effects of overscheduling. And letting our mobile devices rule us.

- If we say "no" to those, we can say "yes" to the important things that have lasting influence, like taking time to be in God's Word so we can get filled with the knowledge of His will for our lives.

- Ask the Lord to help you determine what is truly important in your life and to make pre-decisions—decisions you make in advance that will help you to resist the tyranny of the urgent infection in your life. The goal is that you would live a life worthy of the Lord and please Him in every way. Colossians 1:9-10.

WHAT MIGHT HAPPEN WHEN YOU RESIST THIS "TYRANNY OF THE URGENT" INFECTION?

- Some things will be left unfinished.

- Some events you just won't attend; some tasks you just won't take on.

- Some people might get mad at you.

- Other events you will attend or tasks you will take on.

- Some new friendships will be made.

JESUS SHOWS US HOW TO DO THIS.

- Because of the freedom that Christ gives you through His Spirit and His Word, you don't have to become a slave to the tyranny of the urgent infection.

- Jesus modeled for us how to do this.

  "I must proclaim the good news of the kingdom of God to the other towns also, because that is why I was sent." (Luke 4:42-43)

  "I have brought You glory on earth by completing the work You gave me to do." (John 17:4)

- If Jesus could say no to needy people and good works because He had another purpose, so can you. Jesus did what He was supposed to do not what everyone wanted Him to do. This completed the work God had for Him. The final work came the next day when He gave Himself as the sacrifice for our sins.

The "Tyranny of the Urgent" infection is hollow and deceptive. It leads you away from living a life that pleases the Lord in every way. Knowing the truth of God that you have in Jesus Christ gives you an immune system that fights and prevents spiritual infection.

Let Jesus satisfy your heart needs with His truth and His love so you can get well and stay well.

3: Jesus Is Lord over All!

Colossians 1:15-23

DAY ONE STUDY—GET THE BIG PICTURE

Ask the Lord Jesus to teach you through His Word.

What does the Bible say?

Read the Bible passage below (NIV) including verses from the last lesson. Use your own method (colored pencils, lines, shapes) to mark 1) anything that grabs your attention, 2) words you want to understand, and 3) topics you have seen before in this letter. Draw arrows between thoughts that connect.

1 *[9] For this reason, since the day we heard about you, we have not stopped praying for you. We continually ask God to fill you with the knowledge of his will through all the wisdom and understanding that the Spirit gives, [10] so that you may live a life worthy of the Lord and please him in every way: bearing fruit in every good work, growing in the knowledge of God, [11] being strengthened with all power according to his glorious might so that you may have great endurance and patience, [12] and giving joyful thanks to the Father, who has qualified you to share in the inheritance of his holy people in the kingdom of light. [13] For he has rescued us from the dominion of darkness and brought us into the kingdom of the Son he loves, [14] in whom we have redemption, the forgiveness of sins.*

[15] The Son is the image of the invisible God, the firstborn over all creation. [16] For in him all things were created: things in heaven and on earth, visible and invisible, whether thrones or powers or rulers or authorities; all things have been created through him and for him. [17] He is before all things, and in him all things hold together. [18] And he is the head of the body, the church; he is the beginning and the firstborn from among the dead, so that in everything he might have the supremacy. [19] For God was pleased to have all his fullness dwell in him, [20] and through him to reconcile to himself all things, whether things on earth or things in heaven, by making peace through his blood, shed on the cross.

[21] Once you were alienated from God and were enemies in your minds because of your evil behavior. [22] But now he has reconciled you by Christ's physical body through death to present you holy in his sight, without blemish and free from accusation— [23] if you continue in your faith, established and firm, and do not move from the hope held out in the gospel. This is the gospel that you heard and that has been proclaimed to every creature under heaven, and of which I, Paul, have become a servant.

1. What grabbed your attention from 1:15-23?

2. What verses or specific words do you want to understand better?

3. What words or phrases are repeated in this passage? Give verses.

4. What topics (if any) in this passage have we studied in previous lessons? Give verses.

5. **Healthy Living:** From this lesson's passage (1:15-23), choose one verse to dwell upon all week long. Write it in the space below. Ask God to teach you through this verse.

Respond to the Lord about what you learned today.

DAY TWO STUDY

Read Colossians 1:1-23. Ask the Lord Jesus to teach you through His Word.

What does it mean?

Colossians 1:15-20 is called the "Christ hymn" of Colossians We will enjoy this hymn today!

6. List the things said about Christ to show His supremacy.

7. What clues do we get about the heresy (false teaching) being taught in Colosse? (For example, repeated or stressed words or ideas.)

Paul's answer is to emphasize who Jesus Christ is in relation to God, to Creation, and to the Church.

Christ in Relation to God

8. Look up the following verses, then write in your own words the meaning of the phrase "image of the invisible God (verse 15)".

   • John 1:1,14,18—

   • John 14:9-11—

   • Hebrews 1:3—

   "Image of the invisible God" means:

9. Reread Colossians 1:19. What else is true about Jesus?

10. "Fullness" to the Greek philosophers means "the sum of the supernatural forces controlling the fate of the people." Regarding God, this fullness is the totality of the Divine powers and attributes. "Dwell" means to be permanently at home. If the fullness of God is permanently dwelling in Jesus, what part of God is missing in Jesus?

Christ in Relation to Creation

11. What is revealed about Jesus' relationship to creation in this passage (vv. 15-17)? Be sure to include all the details given.

> **Scriptural Insight:** Christ is the *sustainer* of creation ("hold together," v. 17). Christ is the Person who preserves and maintains the existence of what He has created...Every law of science and of nature is, in fact, an expression of the thought of God. It is by these laws, and therefore by the mind of God, that the universe hangs together, and does not disintegrate in chaos. (*Dr. Constable's Notes on Colossians 2020 Edition,* p. 30)

12. Remembering the people and the purpose for which this letter was written, why do you think Paul expounds on the supremacy of Christ over everything, including the highest orders of the spirit world?

13. To understand Paul's use of the term "firstborn" in verse 15, read Exodus 13:2, 11-15 and Deuteronomy 21:15-17. What were the rights of the firstborn? How does that fit in here?

Focus on the Meaning: Just as the firstborn son had certain privileges and rights in the biblical world, so also Christ has certain rights in relation to all creation—priority, preeminence, and sovereignty (vv. 16-18). (*NIV Study Bible,* p. 1814)

14. From this passage (Colossians 1:15-20), how do we know that "firstborn" cannot mean that Christ was the first created being (a commonly taught error since the second century AD)?

Christ in Relation to the Church

15. Looking at verse 18, what other role does Christ have and why?

Paul uses "firstborn" in verse 18 with a meaning similar to what he uses in 1 Corinthians 15:20, 23 (firstfruits) and Romans 8:29 (the firstborn among many brothers and sisters). Jesus Christ was the first person to rise from the dead never to died again. The term "firstborn" unites His supremacy in the two realms—creation and salvation.

> **Think About It:** The Christ-hymn of Colossians 1:15-20 is a powerful statement about the Person and work of Jesus Christ. Christ's supremacy is seen at every turn. The first portion focuses on His preeminent role in creation, while the second emphasizes His work as Redeemer. To any Christian, in Colosse then or elsewhere today, who may have been or is confused about Christ's role in the world, these six verses testify to Christ's absolute authority, which is not to be shared with any person, angel, or demon. (*Dr. Constable's Notes on Colossians 2020 Edition,* p. 34)

16. ***Deeper Discoveries (optional):*** Read aloud these three other "Christ hymns" found in the New Testament written by different authors—John 1:1-5; Philippians 2:6-11 and Hebrews 1:2-4. How are these similar to the one here in Colossians? What, if any, are the differences? Do these confirm that the same information about Jesus is being taught everywhere by all the apostles?

What application will you make for healthy living?

17. Considering everything you have learned about *who Christ is*, how does this affect your faith? In what ways does this change your thoughts and expectations? Think specifically.

Respond to the Lord about what He has shown you today.

Day Three Study

Read Colossians 1:15-23. Ask the Lord Jesus to teach you through His Word.

What does it mean?

18. Concentrating on vv. 20-22, use a dictionary to define the word "reconcile?"

19. According to Colossians 1:21 and Romans 5:10, what was our problem?

> **Scriptural Insight:** It is important to note that people are reconciled to God ("to Himself") not that God is reconciled to people. For mankind has left God and needs to be brought back to Him. (*The Bible Knowledge Commentary New Testament,* p. 674)

20. From Colossians 1:20-22, what has Christ done for you to solve that problem?

21. How should you respond to the truth that you are completely reconciled to God by your faith in Jesus Christ? (Hint: See also Colossians 1:12, 2:7, 3:15, 3:16, and 3:17.)

22. Christ presents believers to God as what (v. 22)? How does that make you feel?

> **From the Greek:** In our English translations, "holy" (German origin) and "sanctified" (Latin origin) are used interchangeably to translate the Greek word *hagios*, meaning "set apart, separate." For the Christian, to be holy or sanctified means to be set apart *from* sin and *to* God as His possession for His exclusive use. Paul refers to the Colossians as "holy" in 1:2 and 1:22. This is our status before God but not always how we live. The Spirit matures holiness in us as we yield to His work in our lives.

23. What is the "hope" from which we are not to be moved (v. 23)? See also 1:5, 13, 14.

> **Focus on the Meaning:** In Lesson 2 and Lesson 3, we have covered three terms related to what Christ has done for you through His finished work on the cross. These are all part of your identity in Christ and the hope to which we are not to be moved (v. 23).
> - **Redemption** = "You have been purchased by the blood of Christ out of slavery to sin and released into freedom."
> - **Reconciliation** = "The barrier of sin has been taken away, and a bridge has been built. You are able to be saved."
> - **Sanctification** (made holy) = "You are set apart as God's possession for His exclusive use."

24. What do these other verses refer to as our "hope"?

- 1 Thessalonians 5:8—

- Titus 2:13—

- 1 Peter 1:3-4—

What promises are included in our hope?

Focus on the Meaning: Biblical hope is not wishful thinking but confident expectation based on the character of God to back up His promises.

25. Reread Colossians 1:23.

   From the Greek: "If" introduces a condition that the writer assumed was true to reality for the sake of his argument (a first class condition in Greek). We could translate it, "Since." Paul assumed his readers would do what he described. (*Dr. Constable's Notes on Colossians 2020 Edition*, p. 36)

   What is your responsibility in order to enjoy the relationship with God you have already received? See also Colossians 2:6-7.

   Focus on the Meaning: Jesus Christ is the supreme revelation of God, and He is sufficient for the deepest experience of life with God. (*The Baker Illustrated Bible Handbook*, p. 859)

What application will you make for healthy living?

26. What are some specific things you do to stay established and firm in your faith and not moved from your hope? What will you trust God to help you do in the future?

27. How does or should the reconciliation (v. 22) that Christ has accomplished for you as a believer affect the way you relate to ...?

   • those closest to you—

   • to your past—

28. **Respond to the Lord:** What did you learn for yourself regarding how truly great our Lord Jesus is? Feel free to express your thoughts using a creative means (poem, prose, song, art).

DAY FOUR STUDY: TRUTH—THE PRESCRIPTION FOR HEALTHY LIVING

Ask the Lord Jesus to teach you through His Word.

Dwell in Truth You Can Know

29. Review the Colossians passage we studied in this lesson. List the truths about God and His relationship to us that we can KNOW.

Humbly Accept the "I Don't Know or Understand"

30. Make note of anything in the Colossians passage we studied in this lesson that you do not understand at this time.

Discern Teaching through the Complete Revelation of God's Word

31. Evaluate something you have read or heard in light of the TRUTH you are learning—books, social media, billboards—things that sound nice and comfy but may actually lead to or be based upon error in biblical thinking. Does anything come to mind that fits with today's lesson? Discern truth from error using the following process.

    - Step #1: Define the terms and issues involved.

    - Step #2: Ask questions and support your answers with Scripture, looking for truth you can know and what you can't know.

    - Step #3: Think of a graceful response to someone holding to that type of thinking.

Using the process suggested above, how would you evaluate this one and prepare a gracious response to a believer who thinks this is our responsibility:

"Save the planet."

Think About It: If we recognized Jesus as Creator and sustainer, we would not have people being controlled by fear. Knowing Jesus as Creator eliminates fear, changes the world, and saves lives. (Wayne Braudrick, "Wonderful" sermon, Frisco Bible Church, 6/28/15)

Respond to the Lord about what He has shown you today.

Recommended: Listen to the podcast "Crush the 'Jesus Is Not Lord over All' Infection" to reinforce what you have learned. Use the following listener guide.

Crush the "Jesus Is Not Lord over All" Infection

In Colossae, one infection was worse than all the others, with the most damaging effects because it was not just error. It was anti-truth!

THE "JESUS IS NOT LORD OVER ALL" INFECTION

Focus on the Meaning: In the New Testament, Jesus is called the Lord Jesus Christ. You see that in Colossians chapter 1 verse 3. Christ is His title. It comes from the Greek word *christos,* which translates the Hebrew term "Messiah" meaning "anointed one." According to Psalm 110 verse 1, the Messiah would sit at the right hand of God and be called Lord. Jesus not only claimed this for Himself but also demonstrated that He was the Son of God who sits at God's right hand. Jesus is the Christ. He is also the Lord. Lord means master.

The false teachers didn't deny that Christ came, but they dethroned Him.

TRUTH FIGHTS AND PREVENTS THIS DANGEROUS INFECTION

In Colossians chapter 1, Paul writes the strongest statement of the supremacy and deity of Jesus as the Christ and the Lord found anywhere in the New Testament! The prescribed treatment for this infection is the truth about Christ in three areas—1) His relationship to God, 2) His relationship to Creation, and 3) His relationship to the Church.

Jesus' Relationship to God

- Jesus is the representation and exact likeness of God. (v. 15)

- All God's fullness (His totality) dwells permanently in Jesus. (v. 19)

Jesus' Relationship to Creation

- Jesus is the firstborn (priority and superiority) over all creation. (v. 15)

  Focus on the Meaning: The word "firstborn" refers to the one who has priority to and superiority over everything that the father owns.

- Jesus created everything in the entire universe as planned by God the Father. (v. 16) When God created the heavens and the earth, Jesus was there with God the Father.

  *"All things were created **by Him**, and apart from Him not one thing was created that has been created." (John 1:1-13, 14)*

- Jesus is the controlling and unifying force in all of nature. (v. 17)

Focus on the Meaning: The phrase "holds together" means "to cohere" like glue holds things together. Hebrews 1:3 says that "Jesus sustains all things by His powerful word."

- Jesus is Lord of Planet Earth. He is the one who will sustain it, not us. Thinking we have to save the planet or even that we can do that is dethroning Christ as Lord over everything.

Jesus' Relationship to the Church

- Jesus created the Church by combining Jews and Gentiles into one body of believers and appointed Himself Head of the Church. (v. 18, Ephesians 2:15)

- Jesus received a new body as the first one resurrected from the dead. (v. 18)

- Jesus reconciled things (on earth and in heaven) to God through His physical death on the Cross. (vv. 20-22)

- So that in everything He might have supremacy. (v. 18)

Conclusion: We can firmly believe that Jesus is the Christ who is God and Lord over everything. In everything, He is to be **the** Lord, not a Lord. **Jesus Christ is the Lord over all.** We must choose to submit to Him as Lord. He deserves it!

WHEN ARE WE MOST SUSCEPTIBLE TO THIS "JESUS IS NOT LORD OVER ALL" INFECTION?

- We are most susceptible when we seek to be satisfied by our own view of God.

- If we want the benefits of His plan, we must enter His plan His way. If we want our heart need for a relationship with God to be satisfied, we must go through Jesus.

A spiritual infection takes you captive to something other than Christ. The "Jesus Is Not Lord over All" infection is not only bad, it is destructive to your faith. Knowing the truth of God that you have in Jesus Christ gives you an immune system that **crushes** this deadly spiritual infection.

Let Jesus satisfy your heart needs with His truth and His love so you can get well and stay well.

4: Christ in You

Colossians 1:24-2:5

DAY ONE STUDY—GET THE BIG PICTURE

Ask the Lord Jesus to teach you through His Word.

What does the Bible say?

Read the Bible passage below (NIV) including verses from the last lesson. Use your own method (colored pencils, lines, shapes) to mark 1) anything that grabs your attention, 2) words you want to understand, and 3) topics you have seen before in this letter. Draw arrows between thoughts that connect.

1 *[21] Once you were alienated from God and were enemies in your minds because of your evil behavior. [22] But now he has reconciled you by Christ's physical body through death to present you holy in his sight, without blemish and free from accusation— [23] if you continue in your faith, established and firm, and do not move from the hope held out in the gospel. This is the gospel that you heard and that has been proclaimed to every creature under heaven, and of which I, Paul, have become a servant.*

[24] Now I rejoice in what I am suffering for you, and I fill up in my flesh what is still lacking in regard to Christ's afflictions, for the sake of his body, which is the church. [25] I have become its servant by the commission God gave me to present to you the word of God in its fullness— [26] the mystery that has been kept hidden for ages and generations, but is now disclosed to the Lord's people. [27] To them God has chosen to make known among the Gentiles the glorious riches of this mystery, which is Christ in you, the hope of glory.

[28] He is the one we proclaim, admonishing and teaching everyone with all wisdom, so that we may present everyone fully mature in Christ. [29] To this end I strenuously contend with all the energy Christ so powerfully works in me.

2 *[1] I want you to know how hard I am contending for you and for those at Laodicea, and for all who have not met me personally. [2] My goal is that they may be encouraged in heart and united in love, so that they may have the full riches of complete understanding, in order that they may know the mystery of God, namely, Christ, [3] in whom are hidden all the treasures of wisdom and knowledge. [4] I tell you this so that no one may deceive you by fine-sounding arguments. [5] For though I am absent from you in body, I am present with you in spirit and delight to see how disciplined you are and how firm your faith in Christ is.*

1. What grabbed your attention from these verses?

2. What verses or specific words do you want to understand better?

3. What words or phrases are repeated in this passage? Give verses.

4. What topics (if any) in this passage have we studied in previous lessons? Give verses.

5. *Healthy Living:* From this lesson's passage (1:24-2:5), choose one verse to dwell upon all week long. Write it in the space below. Ask God to teach you through this verse.

Respond to the Lord about what you learned today.

DAY TWO STUDY

Read Colossians 1:24-2:5. Ask the Lord Jesus to teach you through His Word.

What does it mean?

6. When you hear the word "mystery" (v. 26), what comes to mind?

> **Focus on the Meaning:** The Greek word translated "mystery" means something "previously unknown, but now-revealed truth." The Greeks talked much of "mysteries." Paul takes their very word and uses it for the gospel. This contrasted with the Colossian heretics' notion that a mystery was a secret teaching known only to an exclusive group and unknown to the masses. (*The Bible Knowledge Commentary New Testament,* p. 674)

7. *Deeper Discoveries (optional):* Look up the following verses which represent the New Testament writers' reference to the mysteries of God. Fill out the chart following the example given.

Verse(s)	The mystery revealed	By whom?	To whom?
Example: Matthew 13:10-11	The knowledge of the secrets of the Kingdom of heaven	Jesus	The disciples
Romans 16:25-26			
1 Corinthians 15:50-54			
Ephesians 3:2-6			
Colossians 1:25-27			
Colossians 2:2-3			

8. Looking at Paul's reference to mystery in Colossians 1:26-27 and 2:2-3:

- God's mystery had been what (1:26)?

- What is that mystery now revealed?

> **Scriptural Insight:** The mystery was not *that* Gentiles would be saved but *how* they could be 'fellow-heirs' (Eph. 3:6, KJV), on the same level with Jews, with no middle wall of partition between them (Eph. 2:12-14) ...That God would save "Gentiles" was no new revelation (Isa. 49:6), but that He would dwell in them and deal with them—on the same basis as He did Jews—was new revelation. (*Dr. Constable's Notes on Colossians 2020 Edition*, p. 40)

9. Based on the context of what you have read so far, what may have been the "fine-sounding argument" (2:4) proclaimed by the false teachers at Colosse?

10. What does Colossians 2:2-3 say about that?

> **Focus on the Meaning:** There is no part of Christian teaching that is to be reserved for a spiritual elite. **All the truth of God is for all the people of God**. (F. F. Bruce, *The Epistles to the Ephesians and Colossians*, 219)

11. Reread Colossians 1:24.

> **Focus on the Meaning:** It might have seemed ironical that Paul was in prison, in view of what he had just said about the success of the gospel. Therefore he quickly explained that his afflictions were part of God's plan, and he rejoiced in them. ... He knew his imprisonment would benefit his readers, at least through his ministry to them in this letter, if in no other way. Furthermore he regarded his "sufferings" as what any servant of Christ could expect ("my share on behalf of His body"), in view of

the world's treatment of his Master ("in filling up what is lacking in Christ's afflictions." The Greek work translated "afflictions" is never used in the New Testament for the atoning sufferings of Christ. It is always used of life's tribulations and persecutions. ... The afflictions of Christ are Christ's actual sufferings now. ... When believers suffer, Christ also suffers because He indwells us (cf. Acts 9:4). (*Dr. Constable's Notes on Colossians 2020 Edition*, pp. 37-39)

- Read 2 Corinthians 1:4-9. How do we share in Jesus' sufferings (vv. 5-7)?

- In what ways can suffering benefit you as a Christian (vv. 4, 9)? See also 2 Corinthians 13:4 and Romans 5:3-5.

12. In Colossians 1:25, Paul talks about a commission or stewardship he received from Jesus (Acts 9:15-16 and 26:12-20).

- What was the commission (stewardship) given to Paul from his first days as a Christian?

- Was suffering part of his commission? _____ Did Paul experience suffering while fulfilling his commission? _____ Did he stay true to that commission in spite of suffering? See Colossians 1:25 again. _____

What application will you make for healthy living?

13. Consider any suffering that you have experienced.

- How was that time of suffering beneficial to you or to those around you? Can you now see good that came from it?

- If you are still struggling to see a benefit to suffering, pour out your heart to Jesus and ask Him to help you see some good in it.

Respond to the Lord about what He has shown you today.

DAY THREE STUDY

Read Colossians 1:24-2:5. Ask the Lord Jesus to teach you through His Word.

What does it mean?

14. As you read through the following verses, notice the phrases, "in Him," "by Him," "in Christ," and "through Him." What do these verses say about who you are AND what you have *in Christ?*

    • Romans 5:9—

    • Romans 8:1—

    • 1 Corinthians 1:30—

    • 2 Corinthians 5:17—

    • 2 Corinthians 5:21—

    • Ephesians 1:3—

    • Ephesians 1:13—

    • Ephesians 2:5—

    • Ephesians 2:10—

    • Ephesians 3:12—

15. Why is there so much emphasis on the phrases "in Him," "in Christ," and "through Him?"

Get "The Believers Identity in Christ" list of benefits and the ID card at the end of this book.

---

16. Read Colossians 1:27. As a believer, you are "in Christ." What is also true about you?

_____ _____ _____, _____ _____ _____ _____

What could "the hope of glory" mean? Glean all of Colossians 1 plus 3:4 for your answer.

> **Focus on the Meaning:** Your position *in Christ* is your: Acceptance before God, assurance of salvation, and identity. Christ's presence *in you* is: Life (regeneration), power for living, the basis of a relationship with God, plus promise and hope. The Holy Spirit is called a "deposit" or "down payment" on our salvation, giving assurance of the completion of His work. (Ephesians 1:13-14)

17. Read Colossians 1:22, 29 and Philippians 1:6. The same energy working in Paul is also working in you.

   • Who enables (empowers) you to become "fully mature" in Christ?

   • What part do you have in the process of becoming "fully mature" in Christ? See all of Colossians 1:1-2:6 for your answer.

18. Why does Christ so powerfully work in you? Review Colossians 1:10 and 23 for insight.

> **Think About It:** The entire statement shows that through faith in Christ we can link our life with a source of strength that enables us to rise above our natural limitations. (*Dr. Constable's Notes on Colossians,* p. 32)

19. Reread Colossians 2:1-5. What does Paul want for everyone who has not met him personally (that includes you)?

20. Considering the relationship that Paul has with this church and the main emphasis of his letter, what would be the value of believers being " united in love" (verse 2)?

> **Think About It:** Only a love which penetrates to the heart and wells up from the heart can sustain the sort of unity that Paul sought. (*Dr. Constable's Notes on Colossians 2020 Edition*, p. 45)

21. In what 2 specific things about the Colossian church does Paul delight (verse 5)?

22. Thinking about what you've learned in this lesson, how is Paul "present" with them in spirit though absent from them physically?

What application will you make for healthy living?

23. What difference does knowing about Christ's power in you for your own spiritual maturity make when you are facing everyday life, a difficult day, or a strenuous task? Get specific— think about events in your recent past (like yesterday!!) Remember, dependent living is recognizing your weakness and relying on His power to make you able to do whatever He gives you to do.

Think About It: "Jesus Christ **laid down** His life **for** you so that He could **give** His life **to** you so that He could **live** His life **through** you. That is the gospel! (Ian Thomas, *The Saving Life of Christ)*)

24. ***Respond to the Lord as you meditate on CHRIST IN YOU.*** How does that truth make you feel? _____ How should it impact your life? What habitual attitudes and actions on your part would you like to see CHRIST **in you** change? Just say, "Lord Jesus, I can't do _____ (the change) on my own, but you can in me and through me. I will trust you to do that." Then, watch what He does!

Day Four Study: TRUTH—the Prescription for Healthy Living

Ask the Lord Jesus to teach you through His Word.

Dwell in Truth You Can Know

25. Review the Colossians passage we studied in this lesson. List the truths about God and His relationship to us that we can KNOW.

Humbly Accept the "I Don't Know or Understand"

26. Make note of anything in the Colossians passage we studied in this lesson that you do not understand at this time.

Discern Teaching through the Complete Revelation of God's Word

27. Evaluate something you have read or heard in light of the TRUTH you are learning—books, social media, billboards—things that sound nice and comfy but may actually lead to or be based upon error in biblical thinking. Does anything come to mind that fits with today's lesson? Discern truth from error using the following process.

   • Step #1: Define the terms and issues involved.

   • Step #2: Ask questions and support your answers with Scripture, looking for truth you can know and what you can't know.

- Step #3: Think of a graceful response to someone holding to that type of thinking.

Using the process suggested above, how would you evaluate this one and prepare a gracious response to a believer who thinks this is good thinking:

"Your best stories will come from your struggles…The seeds of your success are in your failures…Your praises will be birthed from your pains…Keep standing…I have never seen a storm last forever…Seasons change…Be encouraged."

Respond to the Lord about what He has shown you today.

Recommended: Listen to the podcast "Reject the Self-Sufficiency Infection" to reinforce what you have learned. Use the following listener guide.

Reject the Self-Sufficiency Infection

WHAT IS THE SELF-SUFFICIENCY INFECTION?

- The Self-Sufficiency infection tells you that you can be strong on your own. You can take complete care of yourself. You don't need to depend on anyone or anything else to be successful in life.

- The areas of your life where you can be infected by self-sufficiency are in your areas of strength—your skills and abilities.

- You must unlearn what you've learned. And, then learn a new way.

CHRISTIANITY IS CHRIST IN YOU

"Jesus Christ laid down His life for you so that He could give His life to you so that He could live His life through you." That is the gospel! (Ian Thomas, *The Saving Life of Christ*)

- Christianity is about Christ—you're saved by Him, reconciled to God through Him, placed under His authority and protection as He is Lord over all. And, it is about "Christ in you."

- Christ in you is being fused with Christ. *Romans 6:5*

- Christ in you is your power to live a life that pleases God.

- Christ in you is the source of all those marvelous treasures that Paul described in Colossians 1 and 2 because the Lord Jesus Christ who is Lord over all is **in you**.

CHRIST IN YOU TEACHES YOU HOW TO LIVE DEPENDENTLY ON GOD MORE THAN ON YOURSELF

- In his humanity, Jesus demonstrated for us the way we should live in dependence on God.

- He laid down His life for you so that He could give His life to you so that He could live that same kind of life through you.

- Many Christians do not enjoy this kind of Christ-directed life because they have a lack of understanding of two **vital** truths that are completely opposite of self-sufficiency:

    Vital truth #1: Christ's finished work on the cross to secure our complete acceptance before God.

    Vital truth #2: "Christ in you" as the dynamic of daily Christian living.

CHRIST IN YOU AS THE DYNAMIC OF DAILY CHRISTIAN LIVING.

- Because of its dependent life, a baby in the womb could say, "For me, to live is Mom." In the same way, we can say, "For me, to live is Christ."

- To live dependently on Christ is relying on His power in you more than on yourself to achieve the purposes of God in your life. Reject self-sufficiency. Accept God-dependency.

  "But this happened that we might not rely on ourselves but on God, who raises the dead." *(2 Corinthians 1:9a)*

WHAT DOES THIS GOD-DEPENDENCY LOOK LIKE?

- God wants you to become a God-dependent woman who will grow and mature in your thinking and behavior, follow His leading and guidance, and submit your strengths and your weaknesses to Him for His purposes in your life.

- Dependent living is how God grows His children. Human parents rear their children to be less dependent on them and more independent. But God grows His children to be *less independent of Him* and **more dependent on Him.**

- God allows things into our lives that force us to live dependently on Him. And, whether we like it or not, whatever He brings into our lives that makes us more dependent upon Him is good for us.

- God gives you more than you can handle so that you will learn to depend on Him more than on yourself. Christ's power in you is like dynamite in you (Colossians 1:29), so much greater than your own.

Dependent Living is not weakness.

- Dependent living is being stronger and having more influence, more success, and more satisfaction than you could ever have through your own efforts.

- Dependent living is acting in obedience to the Word of God, depending on Jesus Christ for the power to do that, and trusting Him with the results.

The Self-Sufficiency infection is an illusion. When you get too confident in your own abilities, you miss out on all the treasure you have because of Christ in you. You set yourself up for failure when you can't perform. You miss out on the joys of growing fully mature in Christ with all the freedom that brings. Reject the self-sufficiency infection by becoming a God-dependent woman instead.

Let Jesus satisfy your heart needs with His truth and His love so you can get well and stay well.

5: Made Alive with Christ

Colossians 2:6-15

DAY ONE STUDY—GET THE BIG PICTURE

Ask the Lord Jesus to teach you through His Word.

What does the Bible say?

Read the Bible passage below (NIV) including verses from the last lesson. Use your own method (colored pencils, lines, shapes) to mark 1) anything that grabs your attention, 2) words you want to understand, and 3) topics you have seen before in this letter. Draw arrows between thoughts that connect.

2 *¹ I want you to know how hard I am contending for you and for those at Laodicea, and for all who have not met me personally. ² My goal is that they may be encouraged in heart and united in love, so that they may have the full riches of complete understanding, in order that they may know the mystery of God, namely, Christ, ³ in whom are hidden all the treasures of wisdom and knowledge. ⁴ I tell you this so that no one may deceive you by fine-sounding arguments. ⁵ For though I am absent from you in body, I am present with you in spirit and delight to see how disciplined you are and how firm your faith in Christ is.*

⁶ So then, just as you received Christ Jesus as Lord, continue to live your lives in him, ⁷ rooted and built up in him, strengthened in the faith as you were taught, and overflowing with thankfulness.

⁸ See to it that no one takes you captive through hollow and deceptive philosophy, which depends on human tradition and the elemental spiritual forces of this world rather than on Christ.

⁹ For in Christ all the fullness of the Deity lives in bodily form, ¹⁰ and in Christ you have been brought to fullness. He is the head over every power and authority. ¹¹ In him you were also circumcised with a circumcision not performed by human hands. Your whole self ruled by the flesh was put off when you were circumcised by Christ, ¹² having been buried with him in baptism, in which you were also raised with him through your faith in the working of God, who raised him from the dead.

¹³ When you were dead in your sins and in the uncircumcision of your flesh, God made you alive with Christ. He forgave us all our sins, ¹⁴ having canceled the charge of our legal indebtedness, which stood against us and condemned us; he has taken it away, nailing it to the cross. ¹⁵ And having disarmed the powers and authorities, he made a public spectacle of them, triumphing over them by the cross.

1. What grabbed your attention from these verses?

2. What verses or specific words do you want to understand better?

3. What words or phrases are repeated in this passage? Give verses.

4. What topics (if any) in this passage have we studied in previous lessons? Give verses.

5. *Healthy Living:* From this lesson's passage (2:6-15), choose one verse to dwell upon all week long. Write it in the space below. Ask God to teach you through this verse.

Respond to the Lord about what you learned today.

DAY TWO STUDY

Read Colossians 2:1-15. Ask the Lord Jesus to teach you through His Word.

What does it mean?

As you read, keep in mind what you have learned about the false teaching affecting the Colossian church so you will recognize the instructions and solutions Paul gives to them.

6. Reread Colossians 2:6-7. In verse 6, what does Paul confirm to them first?

> **Focus on the Meaning:** "Christ Jesus the Lord," [v. 6 NAS] a phrase that Paul used nowhere else, counteracts three false conceptions of the Savior. These are His deity ("Christ") that Judaism denied, His humanity ("Jesus") that Docetists denied, and His sovereignty ("Lord") that many varieties of false teaching denied. (*Dr. Constable's Notes on Colossians 2020 Edition,* p. 48) Note: Docetists believe Jesus did not have a real body, only an appearance of one.

7. As those who have received Christ Jesus the Lord, how are they and us to continue to live in Him by faith (verse 7)?

8. Let's look at these phrases more closely. See how this list matches the way Paul prayed for them to "live a life worthy of the Lord" in Colossians 1:10-12.

    *   What would it look like to be rooted and built up in Christ?

    *   What would it look like to be strengthened (literally "established") in the faith as you were taught?

    *   What would it look like to be overflowing with thankfulness?

9. In Colossians 2:8, Paul agonizes over the very real danger of believers being deluded or led away from God's truth. He issues a "watch out" here so we will take notice. What could take the Colossians (and us) captive as conquered prey?

10. Philosophy is the love and pursuit of wisdom. Based on what you have learned in Colossians so far, how could you recognize "hollow and deceptive philosophy?" See also the "Escape the Cultural Captivity Infection" notes at the end of Lesson One.

> **Scriptural Insight:** True Christian philosophy "take[s] captive every thought to make it obedient to Christ" (2 Corinthians 10:5). ... if one loves wisdom that is not Christ, [she] loves an empty idol. Such a one will be "always learning but never able to acknowledge the truth (2 Timothy 3:7)." (*The Bible Knowledge Commentary New Testament*, p. 677)

11. Human traditions can be good or bad. Based on what you have learned in Colossians, what would be the test of whether a "human tradition," especially a religious one, was good or bad?

12. The phrase "elemental spiritual forces of this world" is a curious one. Read the "Focus on the Meaning." Then, give some examples of philosophies and current trends of thought that are influenced by "elementary spiritual forces of this world."

> **Focus on the Meaning:** The "elemental spiritual forces of this world" are basic elements of religion undergirded by demonic forces and include anything that leads you to believe you can do without God. These spiritual strategies are the same used by Satan with Eve in the Garden of Eden in Genesis 3: "Did God really say...? (v. 1)", "You will not surely die" (v. 4), and "You will be like God" (v. 5). This would also include bondage to "fate." Before Christ, we are subject to those "elemental spiritual forces." But through union with Christ, we die in relation to them and are no longer bound to obey them. (F. F. Bruce, "The Colossian Heresy, Part 3 of Colossian Problems," *Bibliotheca Sacra*, 141, July-September 1984:196, 204-205).

Your examples:

What application will you make for healthy living?

13. How have you been rooted and built up in Christ, strengthened in the faith as you were taught? If not, keep relying on Jesus to teach you as you study Colossians. Your faith will be strengthened through Paul's teaching.

14. Concerning deception:

- What kind of "hollow and deceptive" input into your thoughts are you receiving now or have received in the past that could still be affecting you? Ask yourself about any teaching or influence you have accepted: *"Where does Jesus fit into their thinking, their philosophy?"* Ask someone to pray specifically for you to be released from anything that is taking you "captive."

- How can gratefulness protect you from being deceived (1:11; 2:7)? How does ungratefulness make you vulnerable to deception?

Respond to the Lord about what He has shown you today.

DAY THREE STUDY

Read Colossians 2:6-15. Ask the Lord Jesus to teach you through His Word.

What does it mean?

15. Focus on Colossians 2:9-10. Let's get a grasp of the facts:

- In whom does all the fullness of Deity dwell in bodily form? _____

- What have you been given in Christ? _____

- Who is the head over every power and authority? _____

- Where else has Paul emphasized this in Colossians? _____

- Why is this important?

Focus on the Meaning: The Greek word translated "bodily form" means a physical body. Colossians 2:9 is a clear statement that Jesus is **fully God** and **fully human**.

16. Focus on Colossians 2:11. Circumcision in the Old Testament referred to the physical cutting away of tissue as a sign of being part of the Jewish covenant with God—a symbol of aligning oneself with God. Paul relates that picture of physical circumcision to what happens to every believer spiritually. See also Romans 2:28-29.

    What happens to every believer?

    Focus on the Meaning: The "flesh" is not the skin but is the *unredeemed* portion of our humanity—our bodies and souls through which indwelling sin assaults us. It is also called the earthly nature (Colossians 3:5) and the "old self" (Colossians 3:9; Romans 6:6). The spiritual circumcision cuts off the power of sin from being the dominating influence in our lives.

17. Read Colossians 2:12 and Romans 6:3-6.

    From the Greek: Most of the time, Paul's use of the word "baptism" is about Spirit baptism not water baptism. The Greek word *baptize* translated "baptism" originally meant to dip or overwhelm a selected item (such as dyeing cloth) so that it is permanently identified as different. Water baptism is a picture of what the Spirit does to us.

    We are identified with Christ in what ways?

18. Name everything that God has done for us according to Colossians 2:13-15.

    - Verse 13—

    - Verse 14—

    - Verse 15—

19. ***Deeper Discoveries (optional):*** What does "dead in your sins" mean (v. 13)? See James 4:17 and Ephesians 2:1-10. Can we save ourselves? See James 2:10 and Galatians 3:10.

20. Since Jesus' death was in the past while we live subsequent to that event, how many of our sins were forgiven by Jesus' death on the cross (v. 13)?

21. What was the "charge of legal indebtedness" that was against us and has now been canceled (v. 14)? Look at other translations of this verse to derive your answer.

22. Colossians 2:15 is a curious verse. Reflect on the following quotes then respond below.

> **Scriptural Insight:** The disarming of the angelic "rulers and authorities" probably refers to Christ's defeat of Satan and his evil angelic (demonic) powers by His death and resurrection...The "public display" probably refers to Jesus' disgracing of the powers of evil when He died on the cross, by bearing the sin that was *their* claim and hold on human beings. Christ "triumphed over" Satan's hosts ("them") at the cross (see 2 Cor. 2:14-16). (*Dr. Constable's Notes on Colossians 2020 Edition*, p. 58)

> Jesus, in His own interest (and in the interest of His people) disarmed the principalities and powers, depriving them of their strength...Jesus, by the victory of the cross, turned the tables on His spiritual assailants; their powerlessness, not His, was publicly exposed...Christ has shown Himself to be their Master, and those who are united to Him by faith need have no fear of them. (F. F. Bruce, "Christ as Conqueror and Reconciler, Part 4 of Colossian Problems," *Bibliotheca Sacra* 141, January-March 1984: 298-299)

How does this truth affect you?

What application will you make for healthy living?

23. In Jesus, we have been made complete (Greek = *pleroo* which means "to fill" or "be made full") through identification with Christ.

    • Review: How have you been "brought to fullness" or made "full" in Him (Jesus)? Draw from chapters 1 and 2.

    • Every woman has a built-in desire for love, security, and significance. Do you understand now how Christ can meet those needs in your heart? If not, why not?

Respond to the Lord about what He has shown you today.

DAY FOUR STUDY: TRUTH—THE PRESCRIPTION FOR HEALTHY LIVING

Ask the Lord Jesus to teach you through His Word.

Dwell in Truth You Can Know

24. Review the Colossians passage we studied in this lesson. List the truths about God and His relationship to us that we can KNOW.

Humbly Accept the "I Don't Know or Understand"

25. Make note of anything in the Colossians passage we studied in this lesson that you do not understand at this time.

Discern Teaching through the Complete Revelation of God's Word

26. Evaluate something you have read or heard in light of the TRUTH you are learning—books, social media, billboards—things that sound nice and comfy but may actually lead to or be based upon error in biblical thinking. Does anything come to mind that fits with today's lesson? Discern truth from error using the following process.

- Step #1: Define the terms and issues involved.

- Step #2: Ask questions and support your answers with Scripture, looking for truth you can know and what you can't know.

- Step #3: Think of a graceful response to someone holding to that type of thinking.

Using the process suggested above, how would you evaluate this one and prepare a gracious response to a nonbeliever who thinks this way:

"God wouldn't want me. I'm too dirty, too messy."

Focus on the Meaning: The Greek word translated "holy" originally referred to something dirty that looked worthless until it was washed and made clean. We are washed clean and made beautiful to God.

Respond to the Lord about what He has shown you today.

Recommended: Listen to the podcast "Conquer the Manipulation by Guilt Infection" to reinforce what you have learned. Use the following listener guide.

Conquer the "Manipulation by Guilt" Infection

The two most common false teachings are that Jesus was not God and that salvation is not by faith alone. Therefore, Jesus' death was not sufficient to pay for all your sins and salvation is achieved by your own good works. So, you can never get rid of the guilt of your sin or the guilt of not doing enough good works to achieve salvation. This is the Manipulation by Guilt infection.

WHAT MAKES A WOMAN SUSCEPTIBLE TO THE "MANIPULATION BY GUILT" INFECTION?

> *[They] gain control over gullible women, who are loaded down with sins and are swayed by all kinds of evil desires, always learning but never able to acknowledge the truth. (2 Timothy 3:6-7)*

- Women become susceptible when they are loaded down with guilt from their sins and when they are in a steady search for the latest new thing to satisfy the restlessness in their hearts.

- When you stay firmly rooted in who Christ is and what He finished on the cross for you, you can conquer the manipulation by guilt infection.

CHRIST'S FINISHED WORK ON THE CROSS

As a direct result of Christ's finished work on the cross, our relationship with God is changed because of our faith in Jesus Christ. What Jesus's death on the cross accomplished for us are described by six truths we can know and claim to conquer any infection, especially the Manipulation by Guilt one.

Word of the Cross #1 is Propitiation.

- God's holy wrath against all sin is fully satisfied by Jesus's sacrifice on the cross. Because of that, God is able to extend mercy to every believer in Christ. *Romans 3:25; Romans 5:9*

- There is no longer any sacrifice that anyone can ever do to satisfy God's wrath against sin apart from what Christ has already done. It's done, finished!

- Because you've trusted Christ and are now found in Christ, you can know and live with confidence that God is satisfied, no longer angry at your sin—ever!

Word of the Cross #2 is Reconciliation.

- God restored our broken relationship with Him by reconciling us to Himself through Jesus's death on the cross. Complete reconciliation, never to be broken again. *Colossians 1:20-22*

- God chose to do that out of his love for us. *Romans 5:10*

- Because you've trusted Christ and are now found in Christ, you can know and live with confidence that your relationship with God is restored…no longer broken because of sin and guilt!

Word of the Cross #3 is Redemption.

- Every human being born on this planet is born into bondage to the kingdom of darkness, sin, and the empty way of life we get from human traditions. Colossians 1:13; 2:8; Romans 6.

- Jesus paid the ransom price for you to be released from that bondage. When you trust in Jesus, you become the possession of a loving, merciful God and are able to live a life that pleases God.

- Because you've trusted Christ and are now found in Christ, you can know and live with confidence that you've been released…no longer in bondage to sin and guilt. Forever.

Word of the Cross #4 is Forgiveness.

- God stepped in and did for us what we couldn't do for ourselves. He transferred our sin to a substitute, Jesus, and it was taken away.

  *When you were dead in your sins…God made you alive with Christ. He forgave us **all** our sins, having canceled the charge of our legal indebtedness, which stood against us and condemned us; He has **taken it away**, nailing it to the cross. (Colossians 2:13-14)*

- Once you trust in Jesus Christ, what you've done wrong in God's eyes from the time you were born through the time of your death has been canceled. All of it. Past, present and future.

- Yet, as long as you live in your earthly body, you will sometimes sin. As an already forgiven Christian, the biblical process for dealing with recognized sin is to remember first that your identity is child of God, agree with God that you've sinned against Him, mourn your sin and depend on the Holy Spirit to help you obey God in the future. Then, trust in Him to help you overcome the consequences of any sinful choices you've made in a way that brings glory to Him. That's living a life that pleases the Lord in every way.

- Because you've trusted Christ and are now found in Christ, you can know and live with confidence that you've been forgiven…no longer burdened by your sin and guilt. Cling to this truth.

Word of the Cross #5 is Justification.

- Because of Christ's finished work on the cross, God chooses to give a "not guilty" status to anyone who places their faith in Jesus Christ. Then, you get His righteousness. *Colossians 1:22*

- When God looks on you, He sees His Son's righteousness taking the place of your sin— even your sin after you've been a believer for a long time.

- When you are tempted to think that God could not possibly accept you because of your weaknesses and guilty past, declare this to yourself: "Because of my faith in Jesus Christ, I am declared righteous no longer guilty in God's eyes." That's a fact.

Word of the Cross #6: Sanctification.

- By faith in Jesus Christ, God declares us holy in His sight. His love chooses to do that for us.

- Every believer has also been set apart as God's special, beloved possession for His exclusive use. *Psalm 4:3*

- You are also "being made holy" in your thoughts, words, and actions by the Holy Spirit so that we become in thought and behavior what we are in status—holy as God is holy. Colossians 3

- Because you've trusted in Christ and are now found in Him, you can know and live with confidence that you are set apart by God, for God. In His eyes, you are perfected, no longer flawed.

A spiritual infection takes you captive to something other than Christ. The "Manipulation by Guilt" infection is bad. Knowing and believing these 6 truths about Christ's finished work on the cross will give you an immune system that **conquers** this spiritual infection.

Let Jesus satisfy your heart needs with His truth and His love so you can get well and stay well.

6: Unhealthy Living

Colossians 2:16-23

DAY ONE STUDY—GET THE BIG PICTURE

Ask the Lord Jesus to teach you through His Word.

What does the Bible say?

Read the Bible passage below (NIV) including verses from the last lesson. Use your own method (colored pencils, lines, shapes) to mark 1) anything that grabs your attention, 2) words you want to understand, and 3) topics you have seen before in this letter. Draw arrows between thoughts that connect.

2 *8 See to it that no one takes you captive through hollow and deceptive philosophy, which depends on human tradition and the elemental spiritual forces[a] of this world rather than on Christ.*

9 For in Christ all the fullness of the Deity lives in bodily form, 10 and in Christ you have been brought to fullness. He is the head over every power and authority. 11 In him you were also circumcised with a circumcision not performed by human hands. Your whole self ruled by the flesh was put off when you were circumcised by Christ, 12 having been buried with him in baptism, in which you were also raised with him through your faith in the working of God, who raised him from the dead.

13 When you were dead in your sins and in the uncircumcision of your flesh, God made you alive with Christ. He forgave us all our sins, 14 having canceled the charge of our legal indebtedness, which stood against us and condemned us; he has taken it away, nailing it to the cross. 15 And having disarmed the powers and authorities, he made a public spectacle of them, triumphing over them by the cross.

16 Therefore do not let anyone judge you by what you eat or drink, or with regard to a religious festival, a New Moon celebration or a Sabbath day. 17 These are a shadow of the things that were to come; the reality, however, is found in Christ. 18 Do not let anyone who delights in false humility and the worship of angels disqualify you. Such a person also goes into great detail about what they have seen; they are puffed up with idle notions by their unspiritual mind. 19 They have lost connection with the head, from whom the whole body, supported and held together by its ligaments and sinews, grows as God causes it to grow.

20 Since you died with Christ to the elemental spiritual forces of this world, why, as though you still belonged to the world, do you submit to its rules: 21 "Do not handle! Do not taste! Do not touch!"? 22 These rules, which have to do with things that are all destined to perish with use, are based on merely human commands and teachings. 23 Such regulations indeed have an appearance of wisdom, with their self-imposed worship, their false humility and their harsh treatment of the body, but they lack any value in restraining sensual indulgence.

1. What grabbed your attention from these verses?

2. What verses or specific words do you want to understand better?

3. What words or phrases are repeated in this passage? Give verses.

4. What topics (if any) in this passage have we studied in previous lessons? Give verses.

5. ***Healthy Living:*** From this lesson's passage (2:16-23), choose one verse to dwell upon all week long. Write it in the space below. Ask God to teach you through this verse.

Respond to the Lord about what you learned today.

DAY TWO STUDY

Read Colossians 2:1-23. Ask the Lord Jesus to teach you through His Word.

What does it mean?

> **Scriptural Insight:** Having revealed what believers have in Christ, Paul next pointed out the errors of the false teachers more specifically to help his readers identify and reject their instruction...Sad to say, there are many Christians who actually believe that some person, religious system, or discipline can add something to their spiritual experience. But they already have everything they ever will need in the person and work of Jesus Christ. (*Dr. Constable's Notes on Colossians 2020 Edition,* p. 60)

6. List the ways false teaching has begun to infiltrate the church of Colosse.

LEGALISM is relying on keeping rules to maintain acceptance before God and/or other Christians. Paul began to address the temptation to legalism in vv. 11-14 when he said circumcision of the heart done by Christ in believers is greater than the old practice of cutting the skin. We died with Christ and are raised to new life with Him. Legalism is a **substitute** for Christ.

7. Focus on vv. 16-17. Paul is referring to human religious traditions (Colossians 2:8).

    •   How is your standing before God NOT to be judged?

    •   Why?

8. Never underestimate the impressiveness (or oppressiveness) of *legalism* (part of the elementary principles of the world mentioned in vv. 8 and 20).

    •   Why do you think the Gentiles in the Colossian church would even be tempted by legalism?

    •   Read Hebrews 10:1-8 and Romans 8:1-8. Why shouldn't we revert back to following the religious Law to please God?

Scriptural Insight: The Law God gave to Israel included 3 aspects: civil (how to govern the nation), religious (how to worship a holy God), and moral (how to treat one another). Christ fulfilled all the requirements of the religious law. Though Christians are not under the civil or religious laws given to Israel, God's moral law has not changed and is reinforced in New Testament writings.

9. Who qualifies you in your righteous standing before God? Why? Provide verses from Colossians 1 and 2 to explain your answer.

10. Notice that the "rules" mentioned here were all ethically neutral things. Think of some modern-day examples of legalistic rules that affect Christian churches and their members.

MYSTICISM is reliance on visions, angelic sightings, or supernatural experiences to improve your relationship with God. Paul uses the terms "worship of angels" and "what he has seen" to identify the mysticism that is affecting the Colossians. Mysticism is a **substitute** for Christ.

11. Read Colossians 2:18-19 in 3 different translations on your Bible app or online to get an understanding of how Paul described those who **seek** such visions, angelic sightings, or supernatural experiences and the results in their lives.

   • What they do (verse 18)—

   • What is the result (verse 19)—

12. Our God chooses to appear in visions and dreams to those who are in Christ as well as to those who are not yet His. The timing and manner is His choice. Paul is addressing those who **seek** special visions and supernatural experiences. Why would that happen? What is the true problem? Look back at all of Colossians 1 and 2 to get your answer. Give verses.

13. Read 2 Corinthians 11:13-15. According to these verses, why is it possible for angelic sightings or supernatural experiences to be from a source other than God?

14. Paul used the Greek word translated "false humility (NIV)" twice in this passage (vv. 18 and 23). Read the "Focus on the Meaning" below to see the fruits of false humility.

> **Focus on the Meaning:** False humility is being proud of one's humbleness and unworthiness to go directly to God and to instead seek a mediator whom you think is easier to approach than God—angels or dead religious heroes. Or, you seek supernatural experiences that validate your emotions, making you feel closer to God. Anyone who does have such a supernatural experience can become puffed up with self-conceit because of a sense of importance and elitism. The Colossians heresy included a form of mysticism (seeking "heavenly" visions or experiences) which temped its followers to look on themselves as a spiritual elite...leaving one at risk of being so unbalanced by the experience that one could no longer distinguish truth from error. People who have mystical experiences tend to attach more importance to what they saw or heard in the course of such an experience than to the sober truth of the Word of God. (F. F. Bruce, "The Colossian Heresy, Part 3 of Colossian Problems," *Bibliotheca Sacra,* 141, July-September 1984:200, 202)

- What are the dangers of **seeking** visions or supernatural experiences?

- Who or what is being substituted for Him?

15. Paul says that seeking mystical experiences will disqualify (deprive) you for the prize (reward). Of what are you being deprived? Look carefully for your answer in all of Chapter 2.

> **Think About It:** Don't let anyone put you down because of an experience they have had but you have not.

What application will you make for healthy living?

16. The temptation to mysticism is as true today as it was at the time Paul wrote to the Colossians. If you or someone you hear about claims to see a vision, to encounter an angel, or to have a supernatural experience:

- What should be the **main** message proclaimed in order for it to be a true message from God? Explain your answer.

- What clues would help you recognize that this person (maybe you) is **seeking** a substitute rather than being satisfied with all that she already has in Christ?

- How could you encourage that person to give up her substitutes and cling to what she has in Christ and His Word? If this is you, what should you do?

Respond to the Lord about what He has shown you today.

DAY THREE STUDY

Read Colossians 2:16-23. Ask the Lord Jesus to teach you through His Word.

What does it mean?

ASCETISM is strict self-denial as a means of personal holiness and earning merit with God. This practice is affecting the Colossians. Asceticism is a **substitute** for Christ.

17. Let's focus now on vv. 20-23. What spiritual practice initiated by false teaching does Paul attack next?

18. Focusing on verse 23:

- These "do not's" seem to have the appearance of what? How?

- What does Paul say these spiritual practices of outward performance or compliance can NEVER accomplish (verse 23)?

- Why is that? Refer back to Romans 8:1-8.

- Consider some modern-day examples of this spiritual practice.

> **Focus on the Meaning:** If people practice various forms of abstinence and find their spiritual health improved thereby, that is their own responsibility. But if they make their abstinence a matter of boasting, and if they try to impose it on others, they are wrong. (F. F. Bruce, "The Colossian Heresy, Part 3 of Colossian Problems," *Bibliotheca Sacra,* 141, July-September 1984:205)

19. The word "fraud" is defined as the "intentional perversion of truth in order to induce another to part with something of value or to surrender a legal right" (merriam-webster.com). A fraud presents a **substitute**. Explain how these false teachings are a "fraud" to the full, complete, and pure gospel message (TRUTH v. ERROR) that was first taught to the Colossians.

Think About It: Four harmful teaching emphases of these false teachers are still with us today. The first is "higher" knowledge (Gnosticism) such as so called scientific, archaeological, or paleontological "facts" that contradict Scripture, so called revelations that claim to be on a par with Scripture, and teaching that directly contradicts biblical revelation. The second is the observance of laws to win God's love (legalism). Some examples are: salvation by works, teaching that puts Christians under the Mosaic Law, and teaching that says sanctification comes by keeping man-made rules. The third is the belief that beings other than Christ (angels, "saints," or ancestors) must mediate between people and God (mysticism) or that certain mystical experiences can improve our relationship with God. The fourth is the practice of abstaining from things to earn merit with God (asceticism). Some examples are: fasting to force God's hand, living in isolation to avoid temptation, and self-mutilation to mortify the flesh. (*Dr. Constable's Notes on Colossians 2020 Edition,* pp. 65-66)

What application will you make for healthy living?

20. Genuine Christians can be deceived by false teaching, even teaching concerning Christ. Have you recognized in your study of Colossians so far that you have a concept about God, Christ, salvation, the church or the Christian life that is not based on Scripture, but on man-made tradition or philosophy? Write it (them) down. Now, give that to Jesus and ask Him to help you accept the truth of God's Word alone.

Think About It: When we make Jesus Christ and the Christian revelation only part of a total religious system or philosophy, we cease to give Him the preeminence. When we strive for "spiritual perfection" or "spiritual fullness" by means of formulas, disciplines, or rituals, we go backward instead of forward. Christian believers must beware of mixing their Christian faith with such alluring things as yoga, transcendental meditation, Eastern mysticism, and the like. We must also beware of "deeper life" teachers who offer a system for victory and fullness that bypasses devotion to Jesus Christ. In all things, He must have the preeminence! (*Dr. Constable's Notes on Colossians 2020 Edition,* p. 66)

The treasure we have in Jesus Christ is greater than anything we can **substitute** for Him.

Respond to the Lord about what He has shown you today.

DAY FOUR STUDY: TRUTH—THE PRESCRIPTION FOR HEALTHY LIVING

Ask the Lord Jesus to teach you through His Word.

Dwell in Truth You Can Know

21. Review the Colossians passage we studied in this lesson. List the truths about God and His relationship to us that we can KNOW.

Humbly Accept the "I Don't Know or Understand"

22. From the Colossians passage we studied in this lesson, make note of anything that you do not understand at this time.

Discern Teaching through the Complete Revelation of God's Word

23. Evaluate something you have read or heard in light of the TRUTH you are learning—books, social media, billboards—things that sound nice and comfy but may actually lead to or be based upon error in biblical thinking. Does anything come to mind that fits with today's lesson? Discern truth from error using the following process.

   - Step #1: Define the terms and issues involved.

   - Step #2: Ask questions and support your answers with Scripture, looking for truth you can know and what you can't know.

   - Step #3: Think of a graceful response to someone holding to that type of thinking.

Using the process suggested above, evaluate and consider gracious responses to people who pray to saints—Joseph, Andrew, Francis, etc.

Respond to the Lord about what He has shown you today.

Recommended: Listen to the podcast "Flee the Spiritual Substitutes Infection" to reinforce what you have learned. Use the following listener guide.

Flee the Spiritual Substitutes Infection

WHAT MAKES US SUSCEPTIBLE TO THE SPIRITUAL SUBSTITUTES INFECTION?

- Whenever you believe that some person, religious system, or discipline can make you feel more spiritual, you've made a substitute for Christ in your life.

- We are called to a person—Jesus Christ—not to a system or to an organization. He is the head of the Church, which is composed of people who belong to Him.

- The treasure we have in the person and work of Jesus Christ is more powerful, more effective, and more valuable than anything we could substitute for Him.

THE CHRIST SUBSTITUTE CALLED LEGALISM

- Legalism is a works-based way of approaching the Christian life. It is taking your faith in Christ and adding other things you must do or not do to gain and maintain acceptance from God and even how to stay saved.

- Legalism does not refer to what is clearly taught in the New Testament about living a life that pleases God and what sin is.

- Legalism is those extra rules that some person or organization has decided you must follow to be a "good Christian" and for God to love you. Whenever God's acceptance of you has an "if you do this" attached to it (other than faith in Jesus Christ), you know you are in the vicinity of legalism.

- Legalism results in straying away from enjoying a love-based relationship with Jesus to practicing a works-based religion with associated bondage to insecurity, guilt, and fear of punishment for not doing it right.

- Jesus died to set you free from that. The Mosaic Law and every other system of works-based religion was nailed to the cross. Jesus Christ took your sin; God gives you His righteousness instead. That's called the Great Exchange.

  God made the one who did not know sin [that's Jesus] to be sin for us, so that in him we [that's you and me] would become the righteousness of God. (2 Corinthians 5:21)

- When God looks on you, He sees His Son's righteousness taking the place of your sin— even your sin after you've been a believer for a long time.

- Legalism is a reliance on self, not Christ. No one can ever be good enough on her own merits to please God. Accept this gift of righteousness by faith. Thank God for it. Flee from any kind of works-based religion that substitutes for the treasure you already have in Jesus Christ.

THE CHRIST SUBSTITUTE OF MYSTICISM

- Mysticism is not when Jesus chooses to reveal Himself unexpectedly to people in dreams or using His Spirit to illuminate your mind and help you understand His Word and give you direction when you ask for it.

- Mysticism is seeking visions, interactions with angels, or supernatural experiences to improve or validate your relationship with God. It is fed by dissatisfaction with what has already been given to us through Christ's finished work on the cross and the complete Word of God that the Holy Spirit uses to teach us how to approach life God's way.

- Mysticism is works-based. It is demanding God to put on a "good show" whenever you want it. It leads to spiritual elitism when you see yourself as being more spiritual than other Christians because God is giving personal messages to you.

- Mysticism also sets Christians up for disappointment and guilt. If God doesn't speak special words to you whenever you ask, then you wonder what you have done wrong. Performance-based religion.

- The danger of mysticism is we have an enemy who always wants to distract us away from Christ. The "nudges," "feelings," intuitions, and random thoughts a person has while emptying one's mind to hear a special word from God every day cannot be put on the same level as Scripture.

- Any teaching that is not centered on the sufficiency of Christ alone to make you acceptable to God is not from God. Any teaching that does not point you to the Bible as being sufficient for you to know God's will and grow spiritually is not from God.

- *Conclusion:* Jesus Christ still speaks, because the Spirit has already spoken. We hold His words in our hands with every printed Bible and every Bible app on our phones and tablets. You can be confident that you are hearing the truth you need to hear. Flee the Christ substitute of mysticism.

Both legalism and mysticism are wrapped up in self—what self wants. Both depend on some kind of experience to validate your faith. Both lead to being puffed up about one's religious life or experiences. Both are spiritual substitutes for Jesus Christ as being supreme in your life. Flee from the Spiritual Substitutes infection. This one will leave you empty.

The Spiritual Substitutes infection is bad. Know that the treasure you have in Jesus Christ is more powerful, effective, and valuable than anything you could substitute for Him. This truth gives you an immune system that **overcomes** any spiritual infection.

Let Jesus satisfy your heart needs with His truth and His love so you can get well and stay well.

7: Living Above

Colossians 3:1-11

DAY ONE STUDY—GET THE BIG PICTURE

Ask the Lord Jesus to teach you through His Word.

What does the Bible say?

Read the Bible passage below (NIV) including verses from the last lesson. Use your own method (colored pencils, lines, shapes) to mark 1) anything that grabs your attention, 2) words you want to understand, and 3) topics you have seen before in this letter. Draw arrows between thoughts that connect.

2 *[19] They have lost connection with the head, from whom the whole body, supported and held together by its ligaments and sinews, grows as God causes it to grow.*

[20] Since you died with Christ to the elemental spiritual forces of this world, why, as though you still belonged to the world, do you submit to its rules: [21] "Do not handle! Do not taste! Do not touch!"? [22] These rules, which have to do with things that are all destined to perish with use, are based on merely human commands and teachings. [23] Such regulations indeed have an appearance of wisdom, with their self-imposed worship, their false humility and their harsh treatment of the body, but they lack any value in restraining sensual indulgence.

3 *[1] Since, then, you have been raised with Christ, set your hearts on things above, where Christ is, seated at the right hand of God. [2] Set your minds on things above, not on earthly things. [3] For you died, and your life is now hidden with Christ in God. [4] When Christ, who is your life, appears, then you also will appear with him in glory.*

[5] Put to death, therefore, whatever belongs to your earthly nature: sexual immorality, impurity, lust, evil desires and greed, which is idolatry. [6] Because of these, the wrath of God is coming. [7] You used to walk in these ways, in the life you once lived. [8] But now you must also rid yourselves of all such things as these: anger, rage, malice, slander, and filthy language from your lips. [9] Do not lie to each other, since you have taken off your old self with its practices [10] and have put on the new self, which is being renewed in knowledge in the image of its Creator. [11] Here there is no Gentile or Jew, circumcised or uncircumcised, barbarian, Scythian, slave or free, but Christ is all, and is in all.

1. What grabbed your attention from these verses?

2. What verses or specific words do you want to understand better?

3. What words or phrases are repeated in this passage? Give verses.

4. What topics (if any) in this passage have we studied in previous lessons? Give verses.

5. *Healthy Living:* From this lesson's passage (3:1-11), choose one verse to dwell upon all week long. Write it in the space below. Ask God to teach you through this verse.

Respond to the Lord about what you learned today.

DAY TWO STUDY

Read Colossians 3:1-11. Ask the Lord Jesus to teach you through His Word.

What does it mean?

Scriptural Insight: Knowing that all wisdom is in Christ (2:1-5), Paul urged the Colossian Christians [and us] to continue in Him (2:6-7), not being deceived by vain philosophies (2:8-10) ...We are not to live under Jewish laws (2:11-17), for that would only rob us of our rewards (2:18-19). We have died with Christ and hence need not submit to legalistic rules (2:20-23). So, we as believers are to seek spiritual values, put off the sins of the old life, and put on the virtues of the new life. This in turn should affect our relationships with other members of our families and society. (*The Bible Knowledge Commentary New Testament,* p. 679)

6. According to 3:1, where is Christ, and what is His role there? See also Ephesians 1:20-23.

From the Greek: The Greek word used at the start of verse 1 when followed by a present tense verb describes something that is totally true, not conditional.

7. What is promised about Christ in verse 4?

8. Based on Colossians 3:1-4, what things are true about you in relation to Christ?

Focus on the Meaning: "'Hidden' implies both concealment and safety; both invisibility and security. [The believer] is not glorified, but he is secure and safe in Christ." (*The Bible Knowledge Commentary New Testament,* p. 680)

9. Colossians 3:1 says, "you have been raised with Christ." Read Colossians 1:13; Romans 6:3-10 and Ephesians 2:4-7. What is the meaning of "raised with Christ?"

10. Because of your position of being "raised with Christ,"

    *   How are you to set your heart and mind?

    *   Based on what you learned in Colossians 2, what does Paul mean by "earthly things" (give verses)?

- Based on what you learned so far in Colossians 1 and 2, what do you think it means to set your heart and mind on "things above?" See also Romans 8:5.

- Why is it necessary to set your heart and mind on things above?

> **Focus on the Meaning:** ...from now on the Christian will see everything in the light and against the background of eternity. He will no longer live as if this world was all that mattered; he will see this world against the background of the larger world of eternity...He will, for instance, set giving above getting, serving above ruling, forgiving above avenging. The Christian will see things, not as they appear to men, but as they appear to God. (*Dr. Constable's Notes on Colossians 2020 Edition,* p. 69)

What application will you make for healthy living?

11. ***Healthy Living:*** Setting your heart and mind on "things above" doesn't mean that you live with your head in the clouds. It does mean that you live for God and approach life God's way rather than the world's way in the middle of the mess around you. Think of a tough situation you have been facing or expect to face. Now look at that situation as it appears to God. How can you approach that situation God's way rather than the world's way?

Respond to the Lord about what He has shown you today.

DAY THREE STUDY

Read Colossians 3:1-11. Ask the Lord Jesus to teach you through His Word.

What does it mean?

12. Focus on 3:5-7. Because of who you are—died with Christ to sin, made alive with Christ, and now with Christ in you:

- What behaviors (thoughts, words, and actions) are you to "put to death" in your life?

From the Greek: Based upon the original Greek words used for these behaviors— "Immorality" refers to illicit sexual intercourse. "Impurity" is moral impurity. "Passion" means uncontrolled illegitimate desire, like an inward fire that is kindled in the heart. "Evil desire" refers to reaching out for some forbidden thing to satisfy itself. "Greed" is the desire to have more of anything materialistic, including lust, that disregards the rights of others. It is "the arrogant and ruthless assumption that all other persons and things exist for one's own benefit. Every sin is basically selfishness, the worship of self instead of the worship of God, the substitution of self for Christ, in one's affections (cf. Col. 3:1-3). (*Dr. Constable's Notes on Colossians 2020 Edition*, p. 74)

- What do you think "put to death" means regarding those behaviors?

- Why should you put those behaviors "to death?"

- From what you've learned in Colossians so far, where do you get the ability to put those behaviors "to death?"

Focus on the Meaning: God's response to all evil and sin is righteous, holy wrath. We must not project our experience with human anger onto God and assume that "His is the same, only bigger." God's wrath is not a *mood* or a fit of *temper*. God's disposition toward sin and evil is as constant and unrelenting as His love and goodness. He hates and rejects evil in a perfect and holy anger. He will never bend or compromise with it. His own nature demands that He judge it through action.

13. Based on Colossians 3:5-6 and Romans 1:18-20, towards what is His wrath directed?

Focus on the Meaning: Since God's first concern for His universe is its moral health, that is, its holiness, whatever is contrary to this is necessarily under His eternal displeasure. Wherever the holiness of God confronts unholiness, there is conflict: This conflict arises from the irreconcilable natures of holiness and sin. God's attitude and action in the conflict are His anger. **To preserve His creation God must destroy whatever would destroy it.** When He arises to put down destruction and save the world from irreparable moral collapse He is said to be angry. Every wrathful judgment of God in the history of the world has been a holy act of preservation. (A.W. Tozer, *The Knowledge of the Holy*, p. 106)

14. According to Romans 5:9-10, how are believers affected by the wrath of God against all human sin?

Focus on the Meaning: God's holy wrath against sin is fully **satisfied** by Jesus' sacrifice on the cross. **"Propitiation"** (to appease, satisfy) is the term that has been used historically for this. Because God's wrath against all sin is fully satisfied by what Jesus finished on the cross, God is able to extend mercy without compromise with evil. This is truth for you to know and claim. Because you have trusted Christ and are now found in Christ, God is no longer angry at your sin—ever! So, how does knowing that truth make you feel? God still uses consequences to draw us away from our sin and back to Him, though.

According to Colossians 3:8-10, you as a believer should also remove from your life anger rage, malice, slander, filthy language, and lying. Let us take each one of those and define them.

15. ANGER. Anger is a normal human emotion designed by God to alert us to something wrong so we will take action against it.

- Look at the dictionary definitions of anger.

- Is all anger wrong? If not, which aspect of anger seems to fit the context of Colossians 3?

- If we are to reflect God on earth, when is anger appropriate?

- But even appropriate anger is a slippery slope. What can easily happen with unresolved anger?

16. RAGE. Define rage. Why is rage something that needs to be "put to death?"

17. MALICE. Define malice. How can malice be related to anger and rage?

18. SLANDER. Define slander. How is slander related to malice?

19. FILTHY LANGUAGE. The Greek word used here (meaning "foul speaking, low and obscene speech") is elsewhere translated as abusive speech. What qualifies as abusive speech or filthy language? See also Ephesians 4:29 and 5:4. Why should you stop it?

20. LYING. Define what it means to stop lying to one another. Would such a command as "do not lie" include exaggeration or embellishment? If so, under what circumstances?

> **Scriptural Insight:** The imperative command against lying is very strong. Paul said to never lie. The reason given (v. 9) applies to all the preceding activities. The "old self" is the person the Christian was before God united him or her with Christ. (*Dr. Constable's Notes on Colossians 2020 Edition,* p. 76)

21. Why is it necessary for the believer to "put off" such behaviors? Look at all of Colossians 3:1-10 for your answer (give verses).

> **Think About It:** Become in experience what you already ARE by God's grace. (*Ryrie Study Bible,* notes on Colossians 3:1-2)

22. How does being renewed in knowledge in the image of your Creator (v. 10) tie in with Genesis 1:26-27 and Genesis 3? See also Romans 8:29 and 2 Corinthians 3:18 and 5:17.

> **Focus on the Meaning: Sanctification** (made **holy**)— Set apart as God's possession for His exclusive use. Believers are made holy by Christ's death on the cross in their relational status before God. Believers are also "being made holy" in their thoughts, words, and actions by the work of the Holy Spirit. This is ongoing from the moment of salvation until the Lord comes or the believer dies when our "being made holy" is complete.

23. Reread Colossians 3:11. Based on what you have learned in Colossians thus far (1:1-3:10), why are all racial, religious, social, and sexual distinctions removed in Christ?

Historical Insight: Jews regarded all others as Gentiles. Greeks and Romans regarded all others as barbarians. Scythians were considered the most barbarous of barbarians—wild, savage nomads. (A. T. Robertson, *Word Pictures of the New Testament*)

24. ***Deeper Discoveries (optional):*** Read Ephesians 2:11-22.

- Why was Colossians 3:11 such an astounding concept for men and women of the New Testament world to hear?

- How important is it to you today?

  Scriptural Insight: There is no national or racial distinction that determines one's acceptability to God nor is there any religious, cultural, or social distinction. Jesus Christ is essentially all that we need for new birth and growth. He indwells every believer and permeates all the relationships of life. (*Dr. Constable's Notes on Colossians 2020 Edition,* p. 76)

What application will you make for healthy living?

25. To put to death the behaviors that do not fit with your life hidden in Christ, you need to be able to recognize them first. Considering what you have studied today in Colossians 3:5-9, do you recognize any of these behaviors in your life? Will you put them to death by choosing to say, "NO!" to them and asking Jesus to enable you to keep saying, "NO"?

26. The Bible never talks about races but about tribes and nations instead. We are told in the Bible that we are all of one blood, one flesh descended from Adam. We all have the same color. Some of us have more of it than others. Racism is a human-generated practice to divide people. Do you feel that a particular racial, religious, or ethnic group is inferior to you? Are you willing to put this attitude "to death"?

Respond to the Lord about what He has shown you today.

DAY FOUR STUDY: TRUTH—THE PRESCRIPTION FOR HEALTHY LIVING

Ask the Lord Jesus to teach you through His Word.

Dwell in Truth You Can Know

27. Review the Colossians passage we studied in this lesson. List the truths about God and His relationship to us that we can KNOW.

Humbly Accept the "I Don't Know or Understand"

28. From the Colossians passage we studied in this lesson, make note of anything that you do not understand at this time.

Discern Teaching through the Complete Revelation of God's Word

29. Evaluate something you have read or heard in light of the TRUTH you are learning—books, social media, billboards—things that sound nice and comfy but may actually lead to or be based upon error in biblical thinking. Does anything come to mind that fits with today's lesson? Discern truth from error using the following process.

- Step #1: Define the terms and issues involved.

- Step #2: Ask questions and support your answers with Scripture, looking for truth you can know and what you can't know.

- Step #3: Think of a graceful response to someone holding to that type of thinking.

Using the process suggested above, and after listening to the podcast, how would you evaluate this Facebook meme about karma and prepare a gracious response to a believer who thinks this is biblical:

"What goes around comes around. Keep your circle positive. Do good and good will come to you. We reap what we sow."

Respond to the Lord about what He has shown you today.

Recommended: Listen to the podcast "Delete the Karma Infection" to reinforce what you have learned. Use the following listener guide.

Delete the Karma Infection

DOES KARMA HAVE ANY PLACE IN A CHRISTIAN'S LIFE? OR, IS IT AN INFECTION?

Karma is the idea that how you live this life will determine the quality of life you will have after reincarnation (from the Buddhist and Hindu religions). After death, your soul is reborn into a new body (human or animal) based upon what kind of life you lived. Karma teaches you get what you deserve.

- The concept of reincarnation is opposite of what the Bible teaches. *Hebrews 9:27*

- The western understanding of karma is the idea of cause and effect where whatever you do is returned to you. So, Westerners hold onto this when it comes to wanting revenge on someone who has wronged us. When embraced by Christians, even casually, karma is an infection in our thinking about our life in Christ.

WHAT DOES THE BIBLE TEACH ABOUT GETTING WHAT YOU DESERVE?

- The general principle regarding your moral and spiritual life is that when you choose to live apart from Christ, your life will get messed up.

- There is not a one-to-one correlation between doing something good or bad and getting the exact good or bad reward for it.

- Thankfully, God chooses to give us His mercy. Mercy is not getting what you deserve. Instead of judgment and punishment, God offers us His grace instead.

THE BIBLE TEACHES GRACE, NOT KARMA.

"For by grace you are saved through faith, and this is not from yourselves, it is the gift of God; it is not from works, so that no one can boast." (Ephesians 2:8-9)

- Grace is undeserved favor. It is a gift from God that you don't deserve. You can never deserve it. God extends His mercy to you because of His great love for you. That's the grace. The gift. He desires you to have it. As you can see, it is very different from karma. More like polar opposites.

- We deserve judgment— every one of us— but we get the very life of God instead by just our faith in Christ. And, zillions of wonderful blessings come to us by that one act alone! We just might have to wait to receive some of them until later.

KARMA DETHRONES CHRIST AND OUR LIFE IN HIM

Looking at Colossians chapter 3, we see many reasons why karma is an infection.

- Verse 1 says that you've been raised with Christ. In God's eyes, you are seated with Christ at God's right hand.

- Verse 2 says that you've already died and your life is now hidden with Christ in God. Nothing is better than that. It is a guarantee.

- Verse 4 reminds you that Christ is your life. Not luck. Not karma. Not what others do to you. Not even your own behavior can change that.

- Verse 10 says that you have a new self that is being renewed to look just like Jesus. God's doing that in you. Not karma.

- There is one and only one act in this life that guarantees anyone's destiny after death. It is either placing your faith in Jesus Christ or rejecting Him. It's all about Christ. John 3:16-18; John 5:24.

GRACE LEADS TO JUSTICE, NOT THE REVENGE OF KARMA

- Revenge has no place in the gospel or in a Christian's life. God will take care of justly punishing those who have rejected Him. Romans 12:17-20.

- Jesus calls us as individual believers to respond differently. Instead of meeting evil with equal or greater force, He urges us to meet evil with good, with kindness. Romans 12:21.

- Recognize that a belief in karma can certainly cause fear in someone's life or lead to a hard heart towards others. So, when you know someone is caught up in the belief in karma, you need to have a graceful response ready to point her to the truth. You can simply say, "I am so glad that God doesn't give me what I deserve. I deserve severe judgment for my sin and nothing good at all in light of His goodness. I am so grateful for His grace to me that expresses His kindness to me because of His love for me. It's a much better way to live than to live in fear that I am not good enough or to live in bitterness against those who have mistreated me." That's recognizing Jesus Christ as Lord.

GRACE = YES! KARMA = NO!

Does karma have anything to do with a Christian's life? Absolutely not! Grace and karma are like oil and water. They don't mix. By spreading the karma infection, you actually draw people away from Jesus and His amazing grace and toward something that poorly substitutes for Him. Delete karma from your words and thinking.

A spiritual infection takes you captive to something other than Christ. The Karma infection is bad. Knowing the truth of God's grace that you have in Jesus Christ gives you an immune system that **deletes** this spiritual infection.

Let Jesus satisfy your heart needs with His truth and His love so you can get well and stay well.

8: Evidence of a Thankful Heart

Colossians 3:12-17

DAY ONE STUDY—GET THE BIG PICTURE

Ask the Lord Jesus to teach you through His Word.

What does the Bible say?

Read the Bible passage below (NIV) including verses from the last lesson. Use your own method (colored pencils, lines, shapes) to mark 1) anything that grabs your attention, 2) words you want to understand, and 3) topics you have seen before in this letter. Draw arrows between thoughts that connect.

3 [5] *Put to death, therefore, whatever belongs to your earthly nature: sexual immorality, impurity, lust, evil desires and greed, which is idolatry.* [6] *Because of these, the wrath of God is coming.*[b] [7] *You used to walk in these ways, in the life you once lived.* [8] *But now you must also rid yourselves of all such things as these: anger, rage, malice, slander, and filthy language from your lips.* [9] *Do not lie to each other, since you have taken off your old self with its practices* [10] *and have put on the new self, which is being renewed in knowledge in the image of its Creator.* [11] *Here there is no Gentile or Jew, circumcised or uncircumcised, barbarian, Scythian, slave or free, but Christ is all, and is in all.*

[12] *Therefore, as God's chosen people, holy and dearly loved, clothe yourselves with compassion, kindness, humility, gentleness and patience.* [13] *Bear with each other and forgive one another if any of you has a grievance against someone. Forgive as the Lord forgave you.* [14] *And over all these virtues put on love, which binds them all together in perfect unity.*

[15] *Let the peace of Christ rule in your hearts, since as members of one body you were called to peace. And be thankful.* [16] *Let the message of Christ dwell among you richly as you teach and admonish one another with all wisdom through psalms, hymns, and songs from the Spirit, singing to God with gratitude in your hearts.* [17] *And whatever you do, whether in word or deed, do it all in the name of the Lord Jesus, giving thanks to God the Father through him.*

1. What grabbed your attention from these verses?

2. What verses or specific words do you want to understand better?

95

3. What words or phrases are repeated in this passage? Give verses.

4. What topics (if any) in this passage have we studied in previous lessons? Give verses.

5. **Healthy Living:** From this lesson's passage (3:12-17), choose one verse to dwell upon all week long. Write it in the space below. Ask God to teach you through this verse.

Respond to the Lord about what you learned today.

DAY TWO STUDY

Read Colossians 3:1-17. Ask the Lord Jesus to teach you through His Word.

What does it mean?

6. Reread Colossians 3:12-14.

- Write out verse 12.

- How are you described at the beginning of verse 12?

- How does reading that you are "dearly loved" / "beloved" make you feel?

7. We learned in the last lesson the Bible often likens behavior to a garment, both bad and good. You were instructed to put off bad behaviors. As God's dearly loved children, with what good behaviors are you to now "clothe yourself" (verses 12-14)? [Note: These are also fruit of the Spirit along with Galatians 5:22-23.]

Since we are being renewed into the image of Christ (verse 10) who displayed these virtues in His life, let's understand them and look for examples of each in Jesus' life.

COMPASSION and KINDNESS.

8. Define compassion. Give an example of compassion from Jesus' life.

9. Define kindness. Give an example of kindness from Jesus' life.

10. How are compassion and kindness…

- similar?

- different?

HUMILITY, GENTLENESS, and PATIENCE.

11. Define humility. Give an example of humility from Jesus' life.

12. Define gentleness. Give an example of gentleness from Jesus' life.

13. Define patience. Give an example of patience from Jesus' life.

14. Why would having humility and gentleness help you to have patience?

BEAR WITH one another and FORGIVE one another.

15. To "bear with" one another in this context means to recognize and endure another's faults. It is a great liaison between patience and forgiveness. Give an example of bearing with one another from Jesus' life.

16. Define forgiveness. Give an example of forgiving one another from Jesus' life.

17. According to Colossians 3:13, what are you to forgive? How are you to forgive?

18. How would having compassion, kindness, humility, gentleness, and patience help you to forgive like that?

LOVE.

19. The Greek word translated "love" is *agape,* meaning "unconditional love."

- What is unconditional love?

- What is the opposite of unconditional love?

- Why would unconditional love bind the other 7 virtues (we just covered) in perfect unity?

- Give an example of unconditional love from Jesus' life.

Think About It: Grudges have no place in a Christian's life! Your capacity to love is directly tied to your capacity to get how deeply you have been forgiven. Agree or disagree?

20. List the terms in all of Colossians 3:8-14 that are used to indicate that your WILL must be *actively* involved effecting change.

Think About It: You either choose to live as God's beloved child should live, wearing "clothes" that are always flattering, or you choose to put on the old self and live in reaction to the circumstances around you.

21. Are you left to your own efforts to clothe yourself with these Christ-like behaviors? ___ Who develops these fine qualities in you as you are willing to cooperate? ___ Review what you have learned in Colossians so far (give verses). See also Galatians 5:22-23.

What application will you make for healthy living?

22. Of the good qualities listed in vv. 12-14, choose one that you especially need and tell God you are willing FOR HIM to develop this characteristic of Christ in you. Then, trust Him to do it.

Respond to the Lord about what He has shown you today.

DAY THREE STUDY

Read Colossians 3:12-17. Ask the Lord Jesus to teach you through His Word.

What does it mean?

23. Focusing on vv. 15-17,

- What specific instruction is given in Colossians 3:15?

- Why? See also Romans 14:19.

Focus on the Meaning: The *NIV Study Bible* note says the Greek word translated "rule" means literally to "function like an umpire." When Christians need to make choices, the peace that Christ produces in our hearts should be a determining factor. We should choose what would result in peace between us and God, and between us and one another, if such a course of action lies within God's moral will. (*NIV Study Bible,* p. 1817; *Dr. Constable's Notes on Colossians 2020 Edition*, p. 80)

24. What instruction is given in Colossians 3:16?

25. What would qualify as the word of Christ? See also Colossians 1:5-7, 23; Luke 4:22, 32; John 14:24 and Galatians 1:11-12.

Think About It: Christ's words were recorded by Spirit-guided apostles (John 14:26; 16:13; 20:31). The words of the Bible, God's written Words, are to dwell in believers. That is, by study, meditation, and application of the Word, it becomes a permanent abiding part of one's life." (*The Bible Knowledge Commentary New Testament*, p. 682)

26. Focusing on verse 16, to "dwell" means to inhabit so as to make oneself at home. So, what does it mean to let the word of Christ *dwell in you richly*?

Focus on the Meaning: His Word should be so deeply implanted within us as to permeate our whole being so that we make all decisions and plans in its light. "He who dwells in a house is the master of the house, not just a passing guest." (*Dr. Constable's Notes on Colossians 2020 Edition*, p. 80)

27. The word of Christ is to dwell in you richly so that you can teach and admonish others with wisdom as the opportunity arises.

- Define teach.

- Define admonish.

- What is needed in order to teach or admonish one another in wisdom? Draw your answer from what you've learned so far in this lesson.

28. Write Colossians 3:17.

What would that look like in your life?

Focus on the Meaning: The basic principle is this. We should say all words and practice all deeds in harmony with the revelation of Jesus Christ, namely, under His authority and as His followers. The "name" comprehends everything revealed and known about the person bearing the name. Moreover, we are to do all with thanksgiving to God. (*Dr. Constable's Notes on Colossians 2020 Edition*, p. 83)

29. Reread vv. 15-17. Notice Paul's inclusion of gratitude and being thankful in each verse. Being thankful is so important that Paul has mentioned it 6 times in this short letter (see also 1:12; 2:7; and 4:2). Why do you think Paul continually reminds them (and us) to be thankful?

Think About It: An attitude of gratitude contributes to an enjoyment of spiritual tranquility, whereas grumbling makes for inner agitation. Do you agree or disagree?

30. Discuss the connection between singing psalms, hymns, and spiritual songs and having gratitude (Greek *charis* which means "grace") in your hearts because you understand God's grace towards you.

Scriptural Insight: It has often been noticed that the Colossian passage is parallel with Ephesians 5:18-20. In the latter passage the hymns and songs are the outgrowth of the filling of the Spirit, while in Colossians they are the result of the deep assimilation of the Word of God. In other words, the Word-filled Christian is a Spirit-filled Christian. (*Dr. Constable's Notes on Colossians 2020 Edition*, p. 82)

What application will you make for healthy living?

31. Letting the peace of God rule in your heart is a choice that you must make.

- Do you have a relationship with another believer that is NOT at peace? Is it *your* position that is breaking the peace? How could a firm grasp of Colossians 3:12-14 encourage you to take steps toward establishing peace with this person?

- Describe a scenario when you *did* let the peace of Christ act as an "umpire" in a relationship.

32. Regarding teaching and admonishing:

- *Teaching*— In what ways do you prepare yourself to be able to teach the word of Christ to others? How can you improve in your preparation to teach?

- *Admonishing*— To admonish someone involves risk in a relationship. Do you shy away from admonishing others because of fear of rejection or loss of relationship? How could a firm grasp of Colossians 3:12-14 encourage you to admonish others from the word of Christ?

33. Regarding thankfulness:

- Are you giving thanks frequently to God for the life that He has given you? If not, why not?

- Maybe it's time to make a list of all the good things God has given to you or done for you. Thank Jesus for each one of those things. Feel free to let the gratitude in your hearts overflow in worship to Christ with singing or through any other creative expression.

DAY FOUR STUDY: TRUTH—THE PRESCRIPTION FOR HEALTHY LIVING

Ask the Lord Jesus to teach you through His Word.

Dwell in Truth You Can Know

34. Review the Colossians passage we studied in this lesson. List the truths about God and His relationship to us that we can KNOW.

Humbly Accept the "I Don't Know or Understand"

35. From the Colossians passage we studied in this lesson, make note of anything that you do not understand at this time.

Discern Teaching through the Complete Revelation of God's Word

36. Evaluate something you have read or heard in light of the TRUTH you are learning—books, social media, billboards—things that sound nice and comfy but may actually lead to or be based upon error in biblical thinking. Does anything come to mind that fits with today's lesson? Discern truth from error using the following process.

    - Step #1: Define the terms and issues involved.

    - Step #2: Ask questions and support your answers with Scripture, looking for truth you can know and what you can't know.

    - Step #3: Think of a graceful response to someone holding to that type of thinking.

Using the process suggested above, how would you evaluate this one and prepare a gracious response to a believer who thinks this is biblical:

"Life is short, and God wants me to be happy."

Respond to the Lord about what He has shown you today.

Recommended: Listen to the podcast "Wipe Out the Narcissism Infection" to reinforce what you have learned. Use the following listener guide.

Wipe Out the Narcissism Infection

WHAT DO I MEAN BY THE NARCISSISM INFECTION?

- Narcissism is an unhealthy self-focus centered on promoting oneself to the extent of doing damage to anyone who doesn't bolster one's image.

- This infection is transmitted by any system of thought that teaches people to put their own needs first and to focus on feeling good about themselves.

- You can recognize the narcissism infection when what someone says or does communicates to the world, "It's all about me."

  We do several things to encourage self-centeredness in our society. One is tolerating and even promoting adolescent behavior in adults. Another is dumbing-down the definition of what we consider acceptable youth behavior. Both of these stem from parenting children in a manner that promotes self-centered personal growth. (Ron Newton, *No Jerks on The Job*)

- Narcissism feeds on our natural tendency to let self be our master in life. That's where we are most susceptible to this infection.

THE FLESH FOCUSES ON SELF AND WANTS TO MASTER YOU

- The Bible says that since the time of Adam, we are born with only sinful tendencies and no ability to be continually "good" or righteous on our own.

- What we call "human nature," the Bible calls "the flesh." The flesh is at war with the Spirit of God within us. The flesh focuses on self and wants to master you. The results are ugly. Colossians 3:5-9; Mark 7:20-23.

- Every human being has a master and is a servant to something—either God and His righteousness or sin and its wickedness. No neutral ground. You might think you are your own master, but you're not. Self is really following the voice of master sin within.

JESUS CHRIST SETS YOU FREE FROM THE POWER OF SELF

- All of your life before trusting in Christ, the old slave master sin called the shots. When you believed in Jesus, a greater power moved in—the Holy Spirit. He sets you free from the *power* of that old slave master to become what God intended you to be.

- You are not set free to be your own master. Your options are still to serve self or to serve God. But you are finally dead to sin and self as your **only** master. You are set free to enjoy your new identity and relationship with your new master Jesus Christ. The Holy Spirit is living inside of you, wooing you to live a life that pleases God and away from "self" ruling your behavior.

- Jesus Christ as our Lord sets you free from the power of self, stopping our destructive anger, rage, hate, lies, and other self-centered actions.

JESUS WIPES OUT THE NARCISSISM INFECTION WITH HIS POWER

- Jesus Christ gave His life for you so He could give His life to you so He could live His life through you. That's what He does. Submitting to Jesus Christ to let Him live His life through you wipes out the narcissism infection.

- Christ's power in you enables you to be the person described in Colossians 3:12-17.

- When you are letting Jesus Christ rule in your heart, that is letting Him live His life through you. The results are peace, gratitude, joy, and giving glory to God rather than to yourself. The difference will be obvious in anyone being healed from the narcissism infection.

Jesus Christ is Lord over everything, including your sense of self and your behavior. As Lord over your behavior, He is powerful enough to change your self-centered behavior into others-focused behavior that pleases Him. But you must choose to submit to Him as Lord rather than to yourself. He deserves it! Life is not all about you. It is all about Him. And, He can wipe out the influence of the narcissism infection on you and on me.

A spiritual infection takes you captive to something other than Christ. The Narcissism infection is bad. In fact, it can be deadly to yourself and to others around you. Knowing the truth of God's grace that you have in Jesus Christ gives you an immune system that **wipes out** this spiritual infection.

Let Jesus satisfy your heart needs with His truth and His love so you can get well and stay well.

9: Evidence of a Word-Filled Life

Colossians 3:18-4:1

DAY ONE STUDY—GET THE BIG PICTURE

Ask the Lord Jesus to teach you through His Word.

What does the Bible say?

Read the Bible passage below (NIV) including verses from the last lesson. Use your own method (colored pencils, lines, shapes) to mark 1) anything that grabs your attention, 2) words you want to understand, and 3) topics you have seen before in this letter. Draw arrows between thoughts that connect.

3 *[12] Therefore, as God's chosen people, holy and dearly loved, clothe yourselves with compassion, kindness, humility, gentleness and patience. [13] Bear with each other and forgive one another if any of you has a grievance against someone. Forgive as the Lord forgave you. [14] And over all these virtues put on love, which binds them all together in perfect unity.*

[15] Let the peace of Christ rule in your hearts, since as members of one body you were called to peace. And be thankful. [16] Let the message of Christ dwell among you richly as you teach and admonish one another with all wisdom through psalms, hymns, and songs from the Spirit, singing to God with gratitude in your hearts. [17] And whatever you do, whether in word or deed, do it all in the name of the Lord Jesus, giving thanks to God the Father through him.

[18] Wives, submit yourselves to your husbands, as is fitting in the Lord.

[19] Husbands, love your wives and do not be harsh with them.

[20] Children, obey your parents in everything, for this pleases the Lord.

[21] Fathers, do not embitter your children, or they will become discouraged.

[22] Slaves, obey your earthly masters in everything; and do it, not only when their eye is on you and to curry their favor, but with sincerity of heart and reverence for the Lord. [23] Whatever you do, work at it with all your heart, as working for the Lord, not for human masters, [24] since you know that you will receive an inheritance from the Lord as a reward. It is the Lord Christ you are serving. [25] Anyone who does wrong will be repaid for their wrongs, and there is no favoritism.

4 *[1] Masters, provide your slaves with what is right and fair, because you know that you also have a Master in heaven.*

1. What grabbed your attention from these verses?

2. What verses or specific words do you want to understand better?

3. What words or phrases are repeated in this passage? Give verses.

4. What topics (if any) in this passage have we studied in previous lessons? Give verses.

5. ***Healthy Living:*** From this lesson's passage (3:18-4:1), choose one verse to dwell upon all week long. Write it in the space below. Ask God to teach you through this verse.

Respond to the Lord about what you learned today.

DAY TWO STUDY

Read Colossians 3:12-4:1. Ask the Lord Jesus to teach you through His Word.

What does it mean?

We could never cover marriage and family relationships in the time allowed for this one lesson. The focus of the lesson is how an understanding of the word of Christ in Colossians 3:12-17 should direct (act as umpire) in our relationships in 2 specific relationship spheres—family and workplace—so as to foster peace (Colossians 3:15). The issue for all of chapter 3 is how Christians can live fruitful and useful lives for God in the middle of a messy world. Typical households of Paul's time included husbands, wives, children, slaves, and hired servants.

> **Focus on the Meaning:** This text is discussing one's responses to various situations and relationships. It is not about roles.

6. What overall heart/mind focus from 3:15-17 is repeated in 3:18-4:1?

FOCUS ON FAMILY RELATIONSHIPS

7. Paul assumes the husband and wife are exhibiting the characteristics from 12-17 in their lives. What instructions does Paul give to the Colossians in directing their family relationships (vv. 16-21) when they are doing everything in the name of Jesus?

- To wives—

- To husbands—

- To children—

- To fathers—

Though today's culture includes households headed by women or men without mates and/or children, the principles of Colossians 3:12-17 that lead to maturity in private home relationships such as submitting to one another and loving one another in a family still apply.

Let us start by defining the Greek words used in these verses in the NIV translation. The following definitions come from the various Greek dictionaries on *Blue Letter Bible*.

> Verse 18 "submit"— from a military term meaning "to arrange [as in troop divisions] in a military fashion under the command of a leader." In non-military use, it was "a voluntary attitude of giving in, cooperating, assuming responsibility, and carrying a burden."
>
> Verse 19 "love"— to love dearly, welcome, be fond of
>
> Verse 19 "harsh"—to make bitter, exasperate, render angry or indignant
>
> Verse 20 "obey"—to listen, harken to a command, be obedient to
>
> Verse 21 "embitter"—to stir up, excite, stimulate (in a good sense); or to provoke to anger or discouragement (its use here) by continual agitation and unreasonable demands.

8. Compare submitting and obeying.

   - How are they similar?

   - How are they different? [Note: the admonition for children to obey parents in Colossians 3:20 refers to minors, not adult children.]

9. Give examples of both of those choices from Jesus' life:

   - Obeying His parent(s)—

     Scriptural Insight: Disobedience to parents is designated in the Old Testament as rebellion against God...Jesus set an example for children by obeying His parents Joseph and Mary. Obedience to parents pleases the Lord. (*The Bible Knowledge Commentary New Testament,* p. 683)

   - Submitting to authorities—

10. Read Ephesians 5:1-2, 22-25. What analogy is given for wives submitting to their husbands?

11. Consider what you just read in the previous question. Colossians 3:18 states that wives are to submit "as is *fitting* in the Lord" (NIV).

- Define fitting.

- What could be meant by that phrase?

> **Scriptural Insight:** Submission is an attitude that recognizes the rights of authority. This subjection rests on divinely prescribed authority, not on any inherent inferiority in spirituality, intelligence, worth, or anything else. This is "fitting" in that it is consistent with what God ordained at the creation of the human race (Gen. 2:18; cf. 1 Tim. 2:13). (*Dr. Constable's Notes on Colossians 2020 Edition,* pp. 84-85)

12. How could submission be both a challenge and a benefit to wives? [Note: we will cover limits to submission in a later question.]

What application will you make for healthy living?

13. Consider your family life and relationships:

If you are married:

- Apply the word of Christ presented in Colossians 3:5-17 to your marriage relationship. What do you need to "put off" and "put on?"

- What can you learn from these verses to help you submit to and encourage your husband's authority and responsibility in the family?

Think About It: I heard someone say that the best marriages are those where the husband and wife take a team approach to life. That requires deciding to be teammates, not just two individuals living together. By taking the team approach to life together, the couple seeks team identification (such as having the same surname), team progress, and team success.

If you are unmarried:

- Apply the word of Christ presented in Colossians 3:5-17 to your singleness. What do you need to "put off" and "put on?"

- What can you learn from these verses to help you be content as a single or to help you choose a mate and prepare for marriage?

If you are raising children:

- Apply the word of Christ presented in Colossians 3:5-17 to your parenting. What do you need to "put off" and "put on?"

- How will you submit to the Lord's authority as a parent and nurture obedience to and love for God in your children's hearts?

Respond to the Lord about what He has shown you today.

DAY THREE STUDY

Read Colossians 3:22-4:1. Ask the Lord Jesus to teach you through His Word.

What does it mean?

FOCUSING ON WORK RELATIONSHIPS

Households in most countries no longer consist of slaves doing the bidding of their masters even though there are parts of the world where the slave-master relationship still exists. Yet, the principle of submission to authority can apply to the typical workplace where there is an authority structure.

14. What are the instructions for employees?

- Verse 22—

- Verse 23—

- Verse 24 & 25—

15. What are the instructions for employers (3:25 & 4:1)?

> **Focus on the Meaning:** The phrase "with all your heart" (verse 23, NIV) literally means "out of the soul," i.e., genuine and from within, not merely by outward pretense...If more Christian employees today served their employers with genuine concern and as though they were serving God, quality and productivity would increase dramatically...If employers...today manifested this kind of compassionate and impartial care for their employees, certainly their employees' motivation to work would radically improve. (*The Bible Knowledge Commentary New Testament*, p. 683)

16. What could be the benefit (present and future) of applying Colossians 3:22-4:1 in a workplace environment?

GENERAL RELATIONSHIPS

17. Why is submission to authority in the family, church, government, or workplace often seen as a threat?

18. What is involved in biblical submission to authority? See 1 Peter 2:21-23; 3:1-6.

19. In Colossians 3:20, 22, how do you qualify "in everything?" Are there any limits to submission to authority? See also Acts 5:29 and what you have learned in Colossians.

20. If the other person in the relationship is not doing his/her part, how should you respond based on your understanding of Colossians 3:12-17?

21. Considering what you have learned from Colossians 3:12-17 and other verses in this study, why do you think submission is pleasing to God?

Think About It: Submission to the Lord is saying, "Lord, I want your will more than I want my own way." Is this your heart attitude?

22. **Deeper Discoveries (optional):** Why would obedience to God's commands in Colossians 3:5-17 actually lead to the abolition of slavery?

Historical Insight: Throughout history wherever Christians have constituted a significant segment of the population and have followed Paul's directions here, the slave system has died. (*Dr. Constable's Notes on Colossians 2020 Edition,* p. 90)

What application will you make for healthy living?

23. Thinking specifically about Colossians 3:19, 23-24, apply these verses to other areas of your life besides a workplace environment. How would following the word of Christ in these verses benefit your children, your volunteer service, and your general witness to an unbelieving world?

Respond to the Lord about what He has shown you today.

DAY FOUR STUDY: TRUTH—THE PRESCRIPTION FOR HEALTHY LIVING

Ask the Lord Jesus to teach you through His Word.

Dwell in Truth You Can Know

24. Review the Colossians passage we studied in this lesson. List the truths about God and His relationship to us that we can KNOW.

Humbly Accept the "I Don't Know or Understand"

25. From the Colossians passage we studied in this lesson, make note of anything that you do not understand at this time.

Discern Teaching through the Complete Revelation of God's Word

26. Evaluate something you have read or heard in light of the TRUTH you are learning—books, social media, billboards—things that sound nice and comfy but may actually lead to or be based upon error in biblical thinking. Does anything come to mind that fits with today's lesson? Discern truth from error using the following process.

    • Step #1: Define the terms and issues involved.

    • Step #2: Ask questions and support your answers with Scripture, looking for truth you can know and what you can't know.

    • Step #3: Think of a graceful response to someone holding to that type of thinking.

Respond to the Lord about what He has shown you today.

Recommended: Listen to the podcast "Counter the 'Work Is Secular' Infection" to reinforce what you have learned. Use the following listener guide.

Counter the "Work Is Secular" Infection

When you're working with your God-given skills, all work can be an act of worship. Not knowing that truth makes you susceptible to the "Work Is Secular" infection.

THE "WORK IS SECULAR" INFECTION

- What are the symptoms?

  Viewing the other 166 hours of your week are second class compared to 2-4 hours of church stuff.

  Viewing work hours as an interruption to "real ministry."

  Viewing work as lacking purpose except to earn income to support the ministry at church.

  Viewing work as something to endure until you can one day do something meaningful (like when you retire and go on the mission field).

- Regarding day to day life, even in secular organizations or industries, there is no "sacred/secular" division in a Christian's life. Jesus Christ is living his life in you and through you 24/7.

- Your time in the weekly worship service, Bible Study, or small group should be your preparation and the stimulus to launch you out into the world—which includes the marketplace—to take the hope of Jesus with you.

WORK IS AN ACT OF WORSHIP, NOT A CURSE.

> *"Whatever you do, work at it with all your heart, as **working for the Lord**, not for human masters, since you know that you will receive an inheritance from the Lord as a reward. It **is the Lord Christ you are serving**." (Colossians 3:23-24)*

- When you are working in an office or on the factory floor, you are serving Jesus Christ with your work.

- Your workplace (be it home, office, factory floor, school room, or road construction) is your mission field.

- Your work environment is where you must intentionally practice letting Jesus live His life through you—in difficult situations, with challenging people, and with integrity honoring the Lord Jesus.

TRUTH TO COUNTER THE "WORK IS SECULAR" INFECTION

- **Truth #1: Work is God's idea.** God created work in the beginning before sin's corruption made it a lot harder to do. Jesus came along to renew us and restore our approach to work as He lives in us and through us. We are free to work for God's glory now.

- **Truth #2: Work is an avenue for accomplishing God's mission.** We are Jesus' ambassadors at work—in the conference room, on the factory floor, at the lunch break, on the playground, and in the kitchen. Work is your mission field and your platform to let Christ live His life through you.

- **Truth #3: Work is the place where God grows us into maturity.** The Spirit of God uses our relationships, successes, failures, and experiences at work as tools in our spiritual growth.

- **Truth #4: Work has purpose beyond ourselves.** God designed work for the good of the world—not just for ourselves. Our work impacts the people in our work environment, our clients, and our managers. We can taste the goodness of God intended for work in the beginning.

- **Truth #5: Work is where we practice depending on Jesus more than on ourselves.** Jesus is Lord over our work. Work is worship, and we glorify Him as we do our jobs well. *Colossians 3:17*

BUT HOW DO WE DO THIS?

- *How do you live out your faith in your workplace?* You do that by being the person described in Colossians 3:12-17. Recognizing Jesus Christ as Lord of your life and your behavior. Letting him live his life through you to invite others around you to want to know him. Ask Jesus to help you do that and trust him to work in you and through you.

- *What is legal to do at work?* Go to firstliberty.org to find out what is legal for a Christian to do in any workplace. You might be surprised by what you can legally do to live out your faith in the marketplace.

- *How do you invest in your co-workers without stealing time from your employer?* You use whatever break time or interaction opportunities you have available to get to know your co-workers and minister to them. Ask Jesus to help you be creative and caring.

- *What if you hate what you do for work?* That's where you submit yourself to Jesus Christ as Lord over you and even over that job. Let him teach you how to be thankful for that work or lead you to something else. Whatever He brings into your life that makes you more dependent upon Him is good for you. Work is a great environment to learn that.

A spiritual infection takes you captive to something other than Christ. The "Work Is Secular" infection is bad. Knowing the truth that work is worship and not a curse gives you an immune system that **counters** this spiritual infection.

Let Jesus satisfy your heart needs with His truth and His love so you can get well and stay well.

10: Making a Difference

Colossians 4:2-18

DAY ONE STUDY—GET THE BIG PICTURE

Ask the Lord Jesus to teach you through His Word.

What does the Bible say?

Read the Bible passage below (NIV) including verses from the last lesson. Use your own method (colored pencils, lines, shapes) to mark 1) anything that grabs your attention, 2) words you want to understand, and 3) topics you have seen before in this letter. Draw arrows between thoughts that connect.

3 *22 Slaves, obey your earthly masters in everything; and do it, not only when their eye is on you and to curry their favor, but with sincerity of heart and reverence for the Lord. 23 Whatever you do, work at it with all your heart, as working for the Lord, not for human masters, 24 since you know that you will receive an inheritance from the Lord as a reward. It is the Lord Christ you are serving. 25 Anyone who does wrong will be repaid for their wrongs, and there is no favoritism.*

4 *1 Masters, provide your slaves with what is right and fair, because you know that you also have a Master in heaven.*

2 Devote yourselves to prayer, being watchful and thankful. 3 And pray for us, too, that God may open a door for our message, so that we may proclaim the mystery of Christ, for which I am in chains. 4 Pray that I may proclaim it clearly, as I should. 5 Be wise in the way you act toward outsiders; make the most of every opportunity. 6 Let your conversation be always full of grace, seasoned with salt, so that you may know how to answer everyone.

7 Tychicus will tell you all the news about me. He is a dear brother, a faithful minister and fellow servant in the Lord. 8 I am sending him to you for the express purpose that you may know about our circumstances and that he may encourage your hearts. 9 He is coming with Onesimus, our faithful and dear brother, who is one of you. They will tell you everything that is happening here.

10 My fellow prisoner Aristarchus sends you his greetings, as does Mark, the cousin of Barnabas. (You have received instructions about him; if he comes to you, welcome him.) 11 Jesus, who is called Justus, also sends greetings. These are the only Jews among my co-workers for the kingdom of God, and they have proved a comfort to me. 12 Epaphras, who is one of you and a servant of Christ Jesus, sends greetings. He is always wrestling in prayer for you, that you may stand firm in all the will of God, mature and fully assured. 13 I vouch for him that he is working hard for you and for those at Laodicea and Hierapolis. 14 Our dear friend Luke, the doctor, and Demas send greetings. 15 Give my greetings to the brothers and sisters at Laodicea, and to Nympha and the church in her house.

16 After this letter has been read to you, see that it is also read in the church of the Laodiceans and that you in turn read the letter from Laodicea.

17 Tell Archippus: "See to it that you complete the ministry you have received in the Lord."

18 I, Paul, write this greeting in my own hand. Remember my chains. Grace be with you.

1. What grabbed your attention from these verses?

2. What verses or specific words do you want to understand better?

3. What words or phrases are repeated in this passage? Give verses.

4. What topics (if any) in this passage have we studied in previous lessons? Give verses.

5. *Healthy Living:* From this lesson's passage (4:2-18), choose one verse to dwell upon all week long. Write it in the space below. Ask God to teach you through this verse.

Respond to the Lord about what you learned today.

DAY TWO STUDY

Read Colossians 4:2-18. Ask the Lord Jesus to teach you through His Word.

What does it mean?

Today we will focus on verses 2-6.

6. Paul gives instruction regarding prayer in verse 2.

- Define devote (v. 2, NIV).

- Remembering the rest of the letter you have already studied, why do you think Paul tells the Colossians to be devoted to prayer, keeping watchful or alert (v. 2)?

Focus on the Meaning: In prayer, we call on God to work, and we express our faith in Him...**The Christian who does not pray is demonstrating independence from God** (cf. John 15:5) ...The accompanying exhortation to 'keep awake, be on the alert' (*gregoreo*) is drawn from the imagery of guard duty (Nehemiah 7:3; Mark 14:34, 37). (*Dr. Constable's Notes on Colossians 2020 Edition*, p. 93)

7. Read verse 2 again.

- How do you think an attitude of thankfulness can make a difference in your prayer life?

- Relate this to what you learned in Colossians 3:15-17.

Scriptural Insight: The repeated emphasis on thanksgiving makes this epistle one of the most "thankful" books in the New Testament (cf. 1:3, 12; 2:7; 3:15-17; 4:2). (*Dr. Constable's Notes on Colossians 2020 Edition*, p. 93)

8. For what two things does Paul ask in Colossians 4:3-4?

9. Why is it so important for Paul, and us, to be able to proclaim the gospel clearly? See also Ephesians 6:19-20.

10. How can we be wise in the way we act toward unbelievers (outsiders)" as Paul states in verse 5? Draw from the following verses to get your answer.

  • Colossians 3:5-17—

  • 1 Thessalonians 4:11-12; 5:14-15—

  • 1 Peter 2:13-17—

  Summary:

  From the Greek: "Act" translates the word *peripateo* meaning to walk as followers of Jesus.

11. What do you think Paul means in verse 5 when he says we should make the most of every opportunity? Give examples.

12. Making the most of every opportunity includes daily conversation with non-Christians (v. 6). What advice does Paul give for our conversation?

13. What does it mean to have your conversation be full of grace, in a sense "seasoned with salt (verse 6)?" Examine what is said in Colossians 3:12-17 and Ephesians 4:29 to derive your answer for the right kind of "salty" language.

> **Focus on the Meaning:** Speech most effectively expresses what is inside the believer. The Christian's speech should mirror the gracious character and conduct of his or her God by demonstrating love, patience, sacrifice, undeserved favor, etc. Salt probably represented both attractiveness, since salt makes food appealing, & wholesomeness, since salt was a preservative that retarded corruption in food...one should wisely suit his or her speech to each need. (*Dr. Constable's Notes on Colossians 2020 Edition*, p. 94)

14. "Know how to answer everyone" doesn't mean you must know ALL the answers because no one does except God. So, what could it mean in light of this context (vv. 2-6)?

What application will you make for healthy living?

15. Is there something that you are especially praying for today? How can you have an attitude of thanksgiving? List at least **three** things for which you can be thankful in your circumstance/situation.

16. Are you praying daily for opportunity to share the gospel with someone? If someone asked you what the "gospel" is, would you be able to tell her?

Read the simple Gospel message below that you could use to share with someone about Christ. Then, write how you would say it to someone.

Has anyone ever explained to you how you can know you're going to heaven? May I?

1. The Bible teaches that God loves all people and wants them to know Him.
2. But people have sinned against God and are separated from God and His love. *Draw a chasm.* This separation leads only to death and judgment.
3. But there is a solution. *Draw bridge.* Jesus Christ died on the cross for our sins (the bridge between humanity and God).
4. Only those who personally receive Jesus Christ into their lives, trusting Him to forgive their sins, can cross this bridge. Everyone must decide individually whether to receive Christ.

Is anything keeping you from trusting Christ right now? Would you like to pray now and tell God you will trust His Son as your Savior?

(from the "Bridge to Life" method of sharing the gospel)

17. Does your speech mirror the gracious character and conduct of your Lord? Ask Jesus to reveal to you any speech that doesn't mirror Him and trust Him to help you replace it with grace-filled speech. Just say, "Lord Jesus, I can't do this on my own. But you can do this in me. I will trust you." Then, watch what He does!

Respond to the Lord about what He has shown you today.

DAY THREE STUDY

Read Colossians 4:2-18. Ask the Lord Jesus to teach you through His Word.

What does it mean?

18. View these names as representing real people with real functions in their world. Beside each name, give Paul's comments about the person and their function in the church / ministry. Follow the cross-references given to see what else is mentioned about them. Add information from online Bible study websites such as www.bible.org. Use all this information to "draw" yourself a word picture about who they were. You will be seeing them in heaven. They may know your name and story so you should know theirs!

- Tychicus (v. 7; Ephesians 6:21-22)—

- Onesimus (v. 8; Philemon 10-11, 15-16)—

- Aristarchus (v. 10; Acts 19:29; 20:4; 27:2; Philemon 23)—

- (John) Mark (v. 10; Acts 12:25; 13:4-5, 13; 15:37-41; Philemon 24; 2 Timothy 4:11; 1 Peter 5:13)—

Scriptural Insight: John Mark, [who wrote the gospel of Mark], is an encouragement to everyone who has failed in his first attempts to serve God. He did not sit around and sulk. He got back into the ministry and proved himself faithful to the Lord and to the Apostle Paul. (*Dr. Constable's Notes on Colossians 2020 Edition*, p. 97)

- Jesus Justus (v. 11)—

- Epaphras (vv. 12-13; Colossians 1:7; Philemon 23)—

Scriptural Insight: Epaphras holds the unique distinction among all the friends and co-workers of Paul of being the only one whom Paul explicitly commended for his intensive prayer ministry. The passage quoted above [4:12-13] may well be called his diploma of success in this ministry. Epaphras' "concern" for the Christians in the other towns near Colosse, "Laodicea and Hierapolis," suggests the possibility that he evangelized these communities as well. (*Dr. Constable's Notes on Colossians 2020 Edition,* p. 98)

- Luke (v. 14; Acts 16:10 where he joins Paul; Philemon 24; 2 Timothy 4:11; wrote the gospel of Luke and book of Acts)—

- Demas (v. 14; 2 Timothy 4:10)—

- Nympha (v. 15)—

- Archippus (v. 17; Philemon 2)—

19. In this passage, we see one of the ways women were very important to the establishment of the early church (assuming Nympha is a woman as some translations say). See also Romans 16:3-5 and 1 Corinthians 16:19. What do you think Nympha's (and Priscilla's) ministry involved for her?

20. How did Paul conclude this beautiful letter?

Scriptural Insight: Paul normally used a secretary to write his letters, and then added a personal word at the end—in his own handwriting—to authenticate his authorship (cf. Rom. 16:22; Gal. 6:11). (*Dr. Constable's Notes on Colossians 2020 Edition*, p. 100)

What application will you make for healthy living?

21. Your home is one of your most valuable assets for ministry. Is your home used in any way for the Lord? If not, why not? What is holding you back?

What happened to the Colossian church?

An earthquake destroyed Colosse shortly after this letter was written. Tacitus recorded that Laodicea was also destroyed in the quake, but was apparently later rebuilt. Colosse lost its importance. Laodicea became the greater city. In Revelation, Jesus wrote a letter to Laodicea, but Colosse was not mentioned because by the mid 90s, Colosse in large part no longer existed. A few people were said to have formed a small village from the ruins of Colosse. The village was totally abandoned in the 8th century.

In the 12th century, the Turks destroyed whatever was left of Colosse. Today Colosse is uninhabited ruins. Motorist guides to Turkey point out Laodicea's ruins but do not even mention Colosse. That may soon change since it is currently being excavated.

Christianity survived in the Lycus Valley until 1923 when the Treaty of Lausanne, ending the Greco-Turkish war, sent Turkish Christians to Greece and Greek Muslims to Turkey.

Respond to the Lord about what He has shown you today.

DAY FOUR STUDY: TRUTH—THE PRESCRIPTION FOR HEALTHY LIVING

Ask the Lord Jesus to teach you through His Word.

Dwell in Truth You Can Know

22. Review the Colossians passage we studied in this lesson. List the truths about God and His relationship to us that we can KNOW.

Humbly Accept the "I Don't Know or Understand"

23. From the Colossians passage we studied in this lesson, make note of anything that you do not understand at this time.

Discern Teaching through the Complete Revelation of God's Word

24. Evaluate something you have read or heard in light of the TRUTH you are learning—books, social media, billboards—things that sound nice and comfy but may actually lead to or be based upon error in biblical thinking. Does anything come to mind that fits with today's lesson? Discern truth from error using the following process.

    • Step #1: Define the terms and issues involved.

    • Step #2: Ask questions and support your answers with Scripture, looking for truth you can know and what you can't know.

    • Step #3: Think of a graceful response to someone holding to that type of thinking.

Respond to the Lord about what He has shown you today.

Recommended: Listen to the podcast "Overcome the 'Holy Huddle' Infection" to reinforce what you have learned. Use the following listener guide.

Overcome the "Holy Huddle" Infection

JESUS COMMISSIONS US WITH A PURPOSE.

Jesus Christ calls you to a new life, clothes you with Himself, commissions you with a purpose, and empowers you to fulfill that purpose. It's a two-fold purpose: to follow Him as His disciple and to live for Him as a disciple-maker.

- To follow Jesus as His disciple means that you make the choice to learn from Jesus through what is taught in the Bible and, in dependent obedience, apply those teachings to your life. We call that discipleship. Inward-focused. Discipleship is incomplete without disciplemaking.

- In disciple-making, you trust in Christ and choose to follow Him as His disciple. The difference is that while you are growing in your own faith, you are also reaching new people for Christ, building them up in their faith, and helping them reach their peers. Outward-focused.

- Disciple-making is intentional and relational. To be intentional means to be deliberate and strategic. You know what relational means—to be together, spending time to listen, talk, know, and be known.

- You know you've caught the "Holy Huddle" infection when you hang out with other Christians so much that you lose connection with those who don't know Jesus and even avoid them.

JESUS SHOWS US HOW TO OVERCOME THE "HOLY HUDDLE" INFECTION.

- Reaching out to nonbelievers takes courage. Jesus demonstrated for us how to be intentional in building relationships with others and introducing them to Him.

- Jesus **engaged** people who needed to know Him throughout his 3½ years of ministry. He did this by **intentionally** going to where the people were who needed to know Him. Wherever He went, He built **relationships** with those who were interested, even those with bad reputations. He invited people to follow Him— some to travel with Him, others to go back home and share about Him. His love for people motivated Him to do this.

- Just like Jesus, we need to build intentional relationships with those who do not know Christ or do not know Him well. To get beyond feelings of inadequacy or fear of rejection, we need to work at preparing ourselves to share about the Lord in daily conversation. Start by asking Jesus to show us how to love the non-Christians in our lives while He works in their hearts.

PRAY AND LOVE THE UNCHURCHED WOMEN IN YOUR LIFE.

- Pray for each one the Lord brings to your mind whenever you think about her, asking the Holy Spirit to work in her heart to draw her to Jesus so she will trust in Him.

- Ask Jesus to give you His love for her and to help you understand what she is feeling and needing from Him. His living through you.

- Commit to make the most of any connection you have to build a relationship with her and show Jesus' love and compassion to her.

- Trust in the Lord to show you how He can use you in her life to introduce her to Jesus.

Only the Holy Spirit can open the eyes of unbelievers to the truth of the gospel and convert their hearts. But Jesus has given us the job to communicate the gospel. We can do our part by praying for them and loving them. We can also be ready to share how Jesus has impacted our lives.

SHAPE YOUR FAITH STORY USING 3 WORDS

- You can shape a short one using just 3 words. Choose any three words to represent your life: one for before knowing Jesus, one for how you came to believe in him, and one for your life as a believer since. Using your three words, create 1-2 sentences for each word—just a brief explanation of how each word relates to your story.

- You can interject your 3-word story into a conversation or ask another woman what 3 words might define her life.

CONSIDER CONVERSATION TRANSITIONS

Be wise in the way you act toward outsiders; make the most of every opportunity. Let your conversation be always full of grace, seasoned with salt, so that you may know how to answer everyone. (Colossians 4:5-6)

- Think through common topics of casual conversation you might have with another woman that could lead to sharing some part of your story.

- Consider how you might identify with her and what God has done in your life to make a difference for you.

KNOW HOW TO SHARE THE GOSPEL FACTS

Choose a simple presentation of the gospel to memorize and have ready to use. Speak it aloud to yourself several times so you know it well without having to think about it. Ask the Spirit to give you boldness and opportunity to share this with someone soon.

JESUS EMPOWERS US TO ACCOMPLISH OUR PURPOSE AS DISCIPLE-MAKERS.

- You and I can be a disciple-maker because Jesus is the one who makes us able. We are simply to obey Him and trust His Spirit to work through us. Being scared is a good thing because we'll rely on Him more. How do you trust Him? Just say, "Lord, I can't, but you can do this in me." Then, watch what He does.

- All of these preparations are interwoven into the Bible study called *Live Out His Love*. You can find it on my website, melanienewton.com, as well as other disciple-making resources.

A spiritual infection takes you captive to something other than Christ. The "Holy Huddle" infection is bad. Knowing the truth that you've been commissioned with a purpose and empowered to accomplish that purpose gives you an immune system that **overcomes** this spiritual infection.

Let Jesus satisfy your heart needs with His truth and His love so you can get well and stay well.

11: Forgiveness and Reconciliation

Philemon 1-25

DAY ONE STUDY—GET THE BIG PICTURE

Ask the Lord Jesus to teach you through His Word.

What does the Bible say?

Read the Bible passage below (NIV) including verses from the last lesson. Use your own method (colored pencils, lines, shapes) to mark 1) anything that grabs your attention, 2) words you want to understand, and 3) topics you have seen before in this letter. Draw arrows between thoughts that connect.

Colossians 4 [17] *Tell Archippus: "See to it that you complete the ministry you have received in the Lord." [18] I, Paul, write this greeting in my own hand. Remember my chains. Grace be with you.*

Philemon 1 [1] *Paul, a prisoner of Christ Jesus, and Timothy our brother,*

To Philemon our dear friend and fellow worker— [2] also to Apphia our sister and Archippus our fellow soldier—and to the church that meets in your home:

[3] *Grace and peace to you from God our Father and the Lord Jesus Christ.*

[4] *I always thank my God as I remember you in my prayers, [5] because I hear about your love for all his holy people and your faith in the Lord Jesus. [6] I pray that your partnership with us in the faith may be effective in deepening your understanding of every good thing we share for the sake of Christ. [7] Your love has given me great joy and encouragement, because you, brother, have refreshed the hearts of the Lord's people.*

[8] *Therefore, although in Christ I could be bold and order you to do what you ought to do, [9] yet I prefer to appeal to you on the basis of love. It is as none other than Paul—an old man and now also a prisoner of Christ Jesus— [10] that I appeal to you for my son Onesimus, who became my son while I was in chains. [11] Formerly he was useless to you, but now he has become useful both to you and to me.*

[12] *I am sending him—who is my very heart—back to you. [13] I would have liked to keep him with me so that he could take your place in helping me while I am in chains for the gospel. [14] But I did not want to do anything without your consent, so that any favor you do would not seem forced but would be voluntary. [15] Perhaps the reason he was separated from you for a little while was that you might have him back forever— [16] no longer as a slave, but better than a slave, as a dear brother. He is very dear to me but even dearer to you, both as a fellow man and as a brother in the Lord.*

[17] *So if you consider me a partner, welcome him as you would welcome me. [18] If he has done you any wrong or owes you anything, charge it to me. [19] I, Paul, am writing this with my own hand. I will pay it back—not to mention that you owe me your very self. [20] I do wish, brother, that I may have some benefit from you in the Lord; refresh my heart in Christ. [21] Confident of your obedience, I write to you, knowing that you will do even more than I ask.*

[22] *And one thing more: Prepare a guest room for me, because I hope to be restored to you in answer to your prayers.*

133

²³ Epaphras, my fellow prisoner in Christ Jesus, sends you greetings. ²⁴ And so do Mark, Aristarchus, Demas and Luke, my fellow workers.

²⁵ The grace of the Lord Jesus Christ be with your spirit.

1. What grabbed your attention from these verses?

2. What verses or specific words do you want to understand better?

3. What words or phrases are repeated in this passage? Give verses.

4. What topics (if any) in this passage have we studied in previous lessons? Give verses.

5. ***Healthy Living:*** From this lesson's passage, choose one verse to dwell upon all week long. Write it in the space below. Ask God to teach you through this verse.

Respond to the Lord about what you learned today.

DAY TWO STUDY

Read Philemon 1-25. Ask the Lord Jesus to teach you through His Word.

What does it mean?

6. To whom is the letter addressed?

7. Why do you think Paul addressed this letter to the church, not just to Philemon?

8. What is Onesimus' relationship to Philemon?

Historical Insight: To help you get the big picture—Onesimus apparently stole some money and ran away from Philemon. He ended up in jail with Paul in Rome. He became a Christian, and now Paul is sending him back to Philemon to restore the relationship. The two men now share the relationship as brothers in Christ as well as master/slave.

9. How does Paul feel about these two men? Give verses to support your answers.

    *   Philemon—

    *   Onesimus—

10. Review Colossians 4:9.

- What is said about Onesimus?

- What is **not** said about Onesimus?

- What could be the reason Paul said what he did about Onesimus in his letter to the Colossians?

11. Back to *Philemon*: What does Paul ask Philemon to do regarding Onesimus?

12. Put yourself in Philemon's shoes. What would be his biggest challenges to accepting Onesimus as an equal in Christ and worshiping alongside him in church?

13. Now, put yourself in Onesimus' shoes. What be his biggest challenges in going back to Philemon and putting himself under Philemon's authority again?

What application will you make for healthy living?

14. Have you been in conflict with someone in your church? Regardless of any feelings of guilt or of being wronged, what challenges did you face (do you face) in loving that person as your sister (brother) in Christ and worshiping alongside them in church?

Respond to the Lord about what He has shown you today.

DAY THREE STUDY

Read Philemon 1-25. Ask the Lord Jesus to teach you through His Word.

What does it mean?

15. If Jesus Christ is above all powers and authorities, in all believers, and is all we need for earth and heaven, His Word should make a difference in our lives in very tough situations. This is a tough situation. The book of Philemon is a practical application of the teachings Paul wrote in his letter to the Colossian church, especially Colossians chapter 3. How should both Philemon and Onesimus apply the teaching Paul gives to the Colossians? Support your answer with verses from Colossians 3:5-4:1.

- Philemon—

- Onesimus—

16. Why should they be obedient to God's teaching through Paul?

Think About It: Freedom of slaves, like all freedom, must come from the heart of Christ-inspired men. Under this compulsion, slavery must ultimately wilt and die. That it took so long for it to do so, that slavery was practiced by many Christians in America until the Civil War ended it, that it is still, in one form or another, in the world today—these humbling facts show the tenacity of socially entrenched sin and the failure of Christendom to deal with it. While all ethical behavior for Christians should arise out of love, rather than regulation or constraint, yet it takes fully committed disciples to put it into practice. (*Dr. Constable's Notes on Philemon 2019 Edition,* p. 20)

17. Read Philemon 11. The name *Onesimus* means "profitable" or "useful." Paul makes use of this in his attempt to persuade Philemon (verse 11). What do you think Paul means?

From the Greek: The name *Philemon* means "affectionate" or "one who is kind." If the slave was expected to live up to his name, then what about the master? (*Constables Notes on Philemon 2019 Edition,* p. 15)

18. In summary, what is Paul really asking of Philemon in this letter regarding Onesimus?

Historical Insight: What happened as a result of this letter? Did Philemon forgive Onesimus? We have no direct record of his response to this letter. However, the fact that Philemon preserved this epistle and allowed it to circulate among the churches, strongly suggests that he *did* behave as Paul had requested. (*Dr. Constable's Notes on Philemon 2019 Edition,* p. 22)

By 110 AD, the bishop of Ephesus was named Onesimus. From some correspondence preserved during this time period, many scholars believe this is the same Onesimus who is the subject of Paul's letter to Philemon.

19. What do you learn from this small but powerful letter about the cost of forgiveness and reconciliation?

What application will you make for healthy living?

20. In Philemon, Paul is proactively serving as a mediator between Philemon and Onesimus.

- Define mediator or to mediate.

- Have you been in a place where you needed mediation between yourself and another person? Maybe you are in that place now. What can you do (based on what you've learned in Colossians and Philemon) to bring about reconciliation?

- Do you need to proactively serve as mediator between 2 people in conflict? What have you learned from Paul's example that you can use to hopefully bring about reconciliation?

Respond to the Lord about what He has shown you today.

DAY FOUR STUDY: TRUTH—THE PRESCRIPTION FOR HEALTHY LIVING

Ask the Lord Jesus to teach you through His Word.

Dwell in Truth You Can Know

21. What 3 truths will you take away from this study of Colossians and Philemon?

Humbly Accept the "I Don't Know or Understand"

22. Remember to accept the things you don't know or understand and patiently wait for the Lord to help you know what He wants you to know.

Discern Teaching through the Complete Revelation of God's Word

23. Remember to evaluate what you read, see or hear in light of the TRUTH you have learned—books, social media, billboards—things that sound nice and comfy but may actually lead to or be based upon error in biblical thinking. Always discern truth from error using the Bible.

Respond to the Lord about what He has shown you today.

Recommended: Listen to the podcast "Defeat the Victim Infection" to reinforce what you have learned. Use the following listener guide.

Defeat the Victim Infection

A SITUATION THAT INCUBATES THE VICTIM INFECTION

- Onesimus had stolen some money from his master and run away. Being led by the Spirit to Paul, the runaway slave heard the gospel and trusted Christ to take away his sins. Paul became his spiritual father, teaching him and loving him as a son.

- Onesimus should return to Philemon his owner and seek forgiveness for stealing the money and for running away. Both men were now Christians.

- Sending Onesimus back to Philemon was the right thing to do. Would the Victim infection overrule the teaching of Christ to forgive and reconcile?

THE VICTIM INFECTION PUTS SELF OVER CHRIST

- When you continually see yourself as a victim of other people's actions or what you think are unfair situations, then you are basically taking over the sovereignty of your life from Jesus Christ as your Lord.

- The victim sees only what is in front of her face not the eternal value. Symptoms of this infection are anger, despair, and self-pity.

- We as Christians can look at a violent incident and say to the victim, "That was gross, black, terrible, straight from the pits of hell and those people are responsible for what they did. But God is bigger and greater. And if you will trust Him, then one day, whether in this life or the next, you will see how He fulfilled that promise to work that bad thing into something good. You choose what to do in the meantime. You can respond by faith now when things aren't ideal, or you can keep being the victim."

- If we truly believe that Jesus Christ is Lord over all, then we must believe that He allows some things in our lives that will draw us to trust Him more as **the** Lord of our lives.

JESUS CHRIST RENEWS OUR HEARTS TO FORGIVE AND RECONCILE

"Renew my heart. We know that Christ is the one who really renews it (NIRV)." Philemon 20

- Jesus Christ renews hearts. To renew means to make something like new again. That involves repairing something broken so that it works well again. That can certainly apply to relationships.

- God's motivation to repair the broken relationship between us and Him was love. God demonstrated His love for us when Christ died for us so that we could be reconciled to Him. When you trust in Jesus Christ, your relationship is renewed. It is no longer broken.

- Through renewed hearts and the shared experience of being Christian brothers, the relationship between Philemon and Onesimus could be restored. But only they could do that with one another and avoid the Victim infection.

- Paul didn't order Philemon to forgive Onesimus. Instead, Paul made him think about it and appealed to him on the basis of love.

- Paul calls Jesus **Lord** 5 times in this short letter. Jesus is not only Paul's Lord but also Philemon's Lord. Lord means master. Philemon has received grace from his master Jesus. A renewed heart is grateful for that forgiveness and grace received. Philemon should, therefore, be a "grace giver" to Onesimus.

CHRIST CALLS US TO BE GRACE-GIVERS TO OTHERS AS WE HAVE RECEIVED GRACE FROM HIM.

Therefore, as God's chosen people, holy and dearly loved, clothe yourselves with compassion, kindness, humility, gentleness and patience. Bear with each other and forgive one another if any of you has a grievance against someone. Forgive as the Lord forgave you. And over all these virtues put on love, which binds them all together in perfect unity. Let the peace of Christ rule in your hearts, since as members of one body you were called to peace. And be thankful. (Colossians 3:12-15)

- Let Jesus Christ be Lord in your life. Ask Him to help you live that kind of life that pleases Him and displays to a watching world that Jesus has renewed your heart. He has forgiven you completely and fills your heart with joy. Jesus gives us His grace so that we can then give grace to others, following His own example.

- A grace-giver does not hold grudges and works at renewing relationships rather than being continually angry with someone. A grace-giver recognizes and submits to the one true master in your life—the Lord Jesus Christ. Ask your Lord Jesus to help you be a grace-giver to your friends, family members, and anyone else who has wounded you. That's how you defeat the Victim infection.

A spiritual infection takes you captive to something other than Christ. The Victim infection will make you very sick. Knowing the truth of God's grace that you have in Jesus Christ gives you an immune system that **defeats** this spiritual infection.

Let Jesus satisfy your heart needs with His truth and His love so you can get well and stay well.

The Believer's Identity in Christ

These descriptions are true for every believer from the moment each person trusts in Jesus Christ for salvation. Cut out the ID card below. Add your name, date/decade of spiritual birth DOB-when you entered this new life: if you know when you believed—day, month, year or decade, and 7 identity traits that are special to you. You are…

1	JUSTIFIED, DECLARED RIGHTEOUS (Rom. 3:23-24)		17	WASHED CLEAN (1 Cor. 6:11)
2	MADE AT PEACE WITH GOD (Rom. 5:1)		18	MADE HOLY AND BLAMELESS (Col. 1:22)
3	SAFE FROM THE WRATH OF GOD (Rom. 5:9)		19	SEALED IN CHRIST (Eph. 1:13-14)
4	RECONCILED TO GOD (Rom. 5:10)		20	CLOTHED WITH CHRIST (Gal. 3:27)
5	REDEEMED (Eph. 1:7)		21	GIVEN CHRIST'S RIGHTEOUSNESS (2 Cor. 5:21)
6	FREED FROM CONDEMNATION (JUDGMENT) (Rom. 8:1; John 3:18)		22	MADE INTO A TEMPLE OF THE HOLY SPIRIT (1 Cor. 6:19)
7	INDWELT BY THE HOLY SPIRIT (Rom. 8:9)		23	MADE PERFECT FOREVER (Hebrews 10:14)
8	ADOPTED AS SONS (Rom. 8:14-15)		24	TRANSLATED OUT OF DEATH INTO LIFE (John 5:24; Eph. 2:1,4-5)
9	ACCEPTED BY GOD (Rom. 15:7)		25	BORN AGAIN (1 Peter 1:3)
10	BAPTIZED INTO CHRIST'S BODY (THE CHURCH) (1 Cor. 12:13)		26	SANCTIFIED (MADE HOLY) (Hebrews 10:10; 1 Cor. 6:11)
11	CHOSEN BY GOD (Eph. 1:4)		27	MADE A NEW CREATION (2 Cor. 5:17; Eph. 2:10)
12	SAVED BY GRACE (Eph. 2:8-9)		28	MADE CHILDREN OF GOD (John 1:12)
13	FREED FROM GOD'S ANGER (1 John 2:2)		29	MADE COMPLETE (Col. 2:9-10)
14	FREED FROM THE LAW (Rom. 7:4)		30	MADE HEIRS OF GOD (Rom. 8:17; Gal. 4:7)
15	TRANSLATED OUT OF DARKNESS INTO LIGHT (Eph. 5:8)		31	MADE CITIZENS OF HEAVEN (Philippians 3:20-21)
16	FORGIVEN (Col. 2:13-14)		32	MADE INTO A HOLY AND ROYAL PRIESTHOOD (Revelation 1:5b-6; 1 Pet. 2:5,9)
			33	GIVEN CONFIDENT ACCESS TO GOD (Eph. 3:12; Hebrews 10:19-23)
			34	WE HAVE BEEN GIVEN EVERYTHING (Eph. 1:3; 2 Peter 1:3)
			35	SECURE IN GOD'S LOVE (Rom. 8:38-39)

MY IDENTITY IN CHRIST

_____, **Child of God, Saint**

DOB: _____

1. _____

2. _____

3. _____

4. _____

5. _____

Small Group Discussion Guide

The following guide is designed for groups that meet for about 1½ hours or less. You will notice that some questions are skipped for the sake of time. These are only suggestions for you.

Ask the group to listen to the first podcast "Truth—The Prescription for Healthy Living" before the first meeting. Help them find it by sending them a link to melanienewton.com/podcasts. Look for Series 3.

INTRODUCTION TO STUDY

It is not necessary to have a separate week for introducing the study. However, it is a good use of time to get to know one another and give them a vision for the study as a whole.

- Start with prayer. Pray for the group to learn from Jesus what He wants them to know and to learn to love one another well to build our community.

- Make sure everyone has a book, a schedule, and Bible / Bible app and knows how to use it. Ask if anyone is new to the Bible and plan to come alongside her during the week.

- Get acquainted with each other. Ask a general question or two such as, "Share your name, where you live, and an activity you enjoy when you have time to do so."

Introduce the study

- Pray: Ask Jesus to teach you through this semester what He wants you to know. Ask Him to help you live with Him as the primary focus of your lives every day.

- Look at the "Contents" page to see the lesson titles.

- Introduction Page 1. Read the top paragraphs and "The Basic Study" section. Draw their attention to the useful study tools at the bottom of the page.

- Page 2: Tell them how to find the podcasts (melanienewton.com/podcasts or any podcast platform—search "Satisfied" by Melanie Newton, Season 3). Or you can read the blogs associated with the podcasts at melanienewton.com/blog. Choose Colossians category then scroll to find the title you want. Read "New Testament Summary" or suggest they do so on their own.

- Read "Discussion Group Guidelines." Add anything else pertinent to your group.

Truth—The Prescription for Healthy Living Podcast

- Read and discuss the listener guide on pages 9-10. Ask questions based on your notes from listening to the podcast ahead of time. From Ephesians 1:17-19, ask them what truth about God they can know.

- Tell them to work on Lesson One for the next meeting. Direct them to the end of Lesson One—Day Four Study. Every lesson will have a "Dwell on truth you can know" question, a "Humbly accept what you don't know" question, and a "Discern all teaching" question. See the examples in Questions 17, 19, and 20.

- **Recommended:** Tell the women to ask the Lord to help them choose a passage (more than one verse) from the Colossians letter to dwell upon / memorize during the semester. Record their passages over the next few weeks.

- Share prayer requests and pray for one another.

LESSON 1: THE GOSPEL RECEIVED (COLOSSIANS 1:1-8)

Choose ahead of time which verses from the questions the group will read aloud as you proceed through the discussion. My recommendations are below.

Start with prayer.

- If you have not already discussed the "Truth—The Prescription for Healthy Living" podcast, do so here. See suggestions above.

Day One Study

- Skip reading the ABC's. Ask Q1.

- Skip reading the "Healthy Living" section and Q2 (to consider personally).

Day Two Study

- Highlight the importance of observation. Ask Q3.

- Qs 4-7. For Q6, the numbers just show emphasis. "In Christ" is the main idea of this letter.

Day Three Study

- *What does it say:* Read Colossians 1:1-2. Ask Qs8-9.

- *What does it mean:* Read Colossians 1:3-8. Ask Q10. Read "From the Greek."

- Skip "Scriptural Insight" and Q11.

- Ask Qs12-13. Do not read the verses in Q13.

- Q14 and "Think About It."

- *What application will you make:* For Q15, break into small groups of 3-4 to share their stories. Give them 5 minutes.

Day Four Study

- Emphasize the meaning of dwell and how that relates to God's truth.

- Qs16-17. Skip reading the verses. Draw out as many truths as possible. Stress how much we can know.

- Qs18-19.

- Skip the "Discern teaching" section if already covered. Go to the podcast listener guide.

- Discuss the podcast. Read the listener guide. Ask questions about understanding and symptoms of the different problems mentioned.

- Read together the italicized paragraph at the end.

- Go back to Q20. Talk about evaluating things they see and hear for the truth or error included in them. Give them an example for the next lesson if you have one from a billboard, social media post, or other source.

- Pray

Recommendation: Listen to a worship song such as "Build My Life."

LESSON 2: A LIFE WORTHY (COLOSSIANS 1:9-14)

Choose ahead of time which verses from the questions the group will read aloud as you proceed through the discussion. My recommendations are below.

Start with prayer.

Day One Study

- Read vv. 9-14. Qs1-4.
- Q5. It is always fun to see what verses your group members especially liked.

Day Two Study

- Reread vv. 9-10. Q6—Discuss the 3 words and the summary. Read "Focus on the Meaning."
- Q7. Read "Focus on the Meaning" first then ask the questions. Read the "Think About It."
- Skip Q8.

Day Three Study

- Reread vv. 10-12. Q9—Go through the chart one area at a time. Draw out as many illustrations as possible. For the "3. being…" section, read "From the Greek" below it to understand the meanings of the words used.
- Q10.
- Read "Think About It." Q11. Skip "Focus on the Meaning."
- Q12—Skip reading the verses. Ask the question though.
- Qs13-14. Skip "Scriptural Insight." Read "Historical Insight." Stress that you are now "in Christ."
- Qs15-16.
- For Q17, break into small groups of 3-4 to share their answers. Give them 5 minutes.
- For your creative ones, ask if anyone has anything to share from Q18.

Day Four Study

- Q19. Give them a minute to write truths especially for those who did not get this far in the lesson. Then share answers. Draw out as many truths as possible. Stress how much we can know.
- Q20.
- Q21. Read the first paragraph and the suggested 3-step process. Ask for comments about the example given. Brainstorm the phrase given.
- Discuss the podcast topic using the listener guide. Ask questions about how this infects us and how to resist.
- Read together the italicized paragraph at the end.

Recommendation: Listen to a worship song such as "In Christ Alone."

LESSON 3: JESUS IS LORD OVER ALL (COLOSSIANS 1:15-23)

Choose ahead of time which verses from the questions the group will read aloud as you proceed through the discussion. My recommendations are below.

Start with prayer.

Day One Study

- Read vv. 13-23. Qs1-2. Skip Qs3-4.
- Q5. It is always fun to see what verses your group members especially liked.

Day Two Study

- Qs6-7. Awesome truth overcomes nonsense.
- Q8. Read the verses only then share answers to what image of the invisible God means.
- Qs9-10.
- Read vv. 15-17. Qs11-12 and "Scriptural Insight."
- Qs13-14. Skip reading verses.
- Read vv. 18-19. Q15, paragraph, and "Think About It." Skip Q16 unless you have time.
- Q17. Break up into small groups of 3-4 to share responses.

Day Three Study

- Read vv. 20-23. Qs18-19 (don't read verses in Q19) and "Scriptural Insight."
- Qs20-22 and "From the Greek."
- Q23 and "Focus on the Meaning."
- Q24. Don't read verses; just answer the question. Read "Focus on the Meaning."
- Q25. Read "From the Greek" and "Focus on the Meaning." Ask Q26.
- Q27—Break into small groups of 3-4 to share answers.
- Q28 if anyone is creative in your group.

Day Four Study

- Q29. Give them a minute to write truths especially for those who did not get this far in the lesson. Then share answers. Draw out as many truths as possible.
- Q30.
- Q31. Evaluate your choice of saying or the one listed in the book. Determine a gracious response to someone who thinks that saying or view is biblical.
- Discuss the podcast topic using the listener guide. Ask questions about how this infects us and how to resist. Read together the italicized paragraph at the end.
- Pray together.

Recommendation: Listen to a worship song such as "What a Beautiful Name It Is."

LESSON 4: CHRIST IN YOU

Choose ahead of time which verses from the questions the group will read aloud as you proceed through the discussion. My recommendations are below.

Start with prayer.

Day One Study

- Read Colossians 1:24-2:5. Qs1-2. Skip Qs3-4.

- Q5. It is always fun to see what verses your group members especially liked.

Day Two Study

- Q6 and "Focus on the Meaning." Skip the chart unless you have lots of time.

- Q8 and "Scriptural Insight."

- Qs9-10 and "Focus on the Meaning."

- Q11. Read verses then "Focus on the Meaning." Read 2 Corinthians 1:4-9. Ask Qs.

- Q12.

- Q13. Break up into small groups to discuss and share prayer need.

Day Three Study

- Q14. Read the verses and state what you have in Christ.

- Q15. Reference "The Believer's Identity in Christ" and ID card in the back of the book. Suggest they do this if they have not already done it.

- Q16 and "Focus on the Meaning."

- Qs17-18 and "Think About It."

- Qs19-22. Skip "Think About It."

- Q23. Break up into small groups to discuss.

- Read "Think About It." Skip Q24.

Day Four Study

- Q25. Give them a minute to write truths especially for those who did not get this far in the lesson. Then share answers. Draw out as many truths as possible.

- Q26.

- Discuss the podcast topic using the listener guide. Draw out what you want to emphasize.

- Q27. Evaluate your choice of saying that fits the lesson or the one listed in the book. Determine a gracious response to someone who thinks that saying or view is biblical.

> Recommendation: Listen to a worship song such as "I Will Follow" by Vertical Worship.

LESSON 5: MADE ALIVE WITH CHRIST

Choose ahead of time which verses from the questions the group will read aloud as you proceed through the discussion. My recommendations are below.

Start with prayer.

Day One Study

- Read Colossians 2:6-15. Qs1-2. Skip Qs3-4.

- Q5. It is always fun to see what verses your group members especially liked.

Day Two Study

- Reread vv. 6-8. Q6 and "Focus on the Meaning."

- Qs7-10 and "Scriptural Insight."

- Qs11-12 and "Focus on the Meaning."

- Q13.

- Q14. First part is personal. Second part: Break up into small groups to discuss the relation between gratitude and vulnerability of deception.

Day Three Study

- Read vv. 9-15. Q15 and "Focus on the Meaning."

- Q16. Read verses and "Focus on the Meaning."

- Q17. Read verses and "From the Greek."

- Qs18, 20, & 21.

- Q22. Ask what grabbed their attention from the "Scriptural Insight." Then, the question.

- Q23. The first part is a review. The second part is personal but can lead to a wonderful discussion.

Day Four Study

- Q24. Give them a minute to write truths especially for those who did not get this far in the lesson. Then share answers. Draw out as many truths as possible.

- Q25.

- Discuss the podcast. Go over each of the six words of the cross which are relationship changers between us and God.

- Q26. Evaluate your choice of saying that fits the lesson or the one listed in the book. Determine a gracious response to someone who thinks that saying or view is biblical.

> Recommendation: Listen to a worship song such as "Lord, I Need You."

LESSON 6: UNHEALTHY LIVING

Choose ahead of time which verses from the questions the group will read aloud as you proceed through the discussion. My recommendations are below.

Start with prayer.

Day One Study

- Read Colossians 2:16-23. Qs1-2. Skip Qs3-4.
- Q5. It is always fun to see what verses your group members especially liked.

Day Two Study

- Skip "Scriptural Insight." Ask Q6.
- Read definition of "legalism." Qs7-8 and "Scriptural Insight."
- Qs9-10.
- Read definition of "mysticism." Read Colossians 2:18-19. Q11 chart.
- Qs12-13. Skip Galatians 1:6-9. Read 2 Corinthians 11:13-15.
- Q14 and "Focus on the Meaning."
- Q15 and "Think About It."
- Q16.

Day Three Study

- Read definition of "asceticism." Read Colossians 2:20-23. Q17. Brainstorm modern examples.
- Q18 and "Focus on the Meaning."
- Q19 and "Think About It." Consider gracious responses to people who pray to saints.
- Q20 and "Think About It."

Day Four Study

- Qs 21-22.
- Discuss the podcast topic using the listener guide. Draw out what you want to emphasize.
- Q23. Evaluate your choice of saying that fits the lesson or the one listed in the book. Determine a gracious response to someone who thinks that saying or view is biblical.

Recommendation: Listen to a worship song such as "In Christ Alone."

LESSON 7: LIVING ABOVE

Choose ahead of time which verses from the questions the group will read aloud as you proceed through the discussion. My recommendations are below.

Start with prayer.

Day One Study

- Read Colossians 3:1-11. Ask Qs1-2—quick answers. Skip Qs3-4. Ask Q5 to see what verses the women liked.

Day Two Study

- Skip reading verses again. Read "Scriptural Insight."

- Q6. Note: Some translations start with "if" rather than "since." The Greek word there followed by a present tense verb describes something that is totally true. Not iffy.

- Ask Q8 first then Q7. Read "Focus on the Meaning." The bad teachers claimed mysterious things were hidden in their secret books. Paul grabbed their special word and used it against them. It is as if he said, "For you the treasures of wisdom are hidden in your secret books. For us, Christ is the treasury of wisdom and we are hidden in Him." Hooray!!

- Qs9-10 and "Focus on the Meaning."

- Q11. Break up into small groups of 3-4 to discuss. Give them 5 minutes.

Day Three Study

- Read vv. 5-7. Ask Q12 but skip "From the Greek." Read "Focus on the Meaning."

- Qs13-14 and both "Focus on the Meaning" sections.

- Read vv. 8-10. Qs15-20—Don't spend much time on definitions. Focus on the question asked.

- Skip "Scriptural Insight" after Q20.

- Qs21-22 and "Focus on the Meaning."

- Read 3:11 and ask Q23. Don't read the "Historical Insight."

- Skip Qs24-26 (the last two are personal). You could do Q25 in small groups if time.

Day Four Study

- Q27. Give them 1 minute to write something down before getting answers.

- Skip Qs28-29. Go to the podcast page.

- Discuss the podcast topic "Karma" using the listener guide. Ask questions based on your own insights and understanding.

- Read together the italicized paragraph at the end.

- Prayer time.

Recommendation: Listen to a worship song such as "Before the Throne of God Above."

LESSON 8: EVIDENCE OF A THANKFUL HEART

Choose ahead of time which verses from the questions the group will read aloud as you proceed through the discussion. My recommendations are below.

Start with prayer.

Day One Study

- Read Colossians 3:12-17. Ask Qs1-2—quick answers. Skip Qs3-4. Ask Q5 to see what verses the women liked.

Day Two Study

- Q6. Skip reading the verse. Ask the next two bullet points.
- Q7. These clothes are always flattering.
- Qs8-14. Do not spend much time on the definitions. Focus on the examples.
- Qs15-18.
- Qs19-21 and both "Think About It" sections.
- Q22. Break up into groups of 2-3. Share answers and pray for one another in that way.

Day Three Study

- Read Colossians 3:15-17 and Romans 14:19. Q23 and "Focus on the Meaning."
- Qs24-25 and "Think About It."
- Qs26-27 and "Think About It."
- Q28. Do not read verse. Answer question. Skip "Focus on the Meaning."
- Qs29-30. Read "Think About It." Skip "Scriptural Insight."
- Qs 31-33. Choose one to break up into small groups for sharing.

Day Four Study

- Q34. Give them 1 minute to write something down before getting answers.
- Skip Qs35-36. Go to the podcast page.
- Discuss the podcast topic using the listener guide. Ask questions based on your own insights and understanding.
- Q36. Evaluate this statement in light of what you learned today. "*"Life is short, and God wants me to be happy."*
- Prayer time.

Recommendation: Listen to a worship song such as "Build Me Life" or "Lord, I Need You."

LESSON 9: EVIDENCE OF A WORD-FILLED LIFE

Choose ahead of time which verses from the questions the group will read aloud as you proceed through the discussion. My recommendations are below.

Start with prayer.

Day One Study

- Read Colossians 3:18-4:1. Ask Qs1-2—quick answers. Skip Qs3-4. Ask Q5 to see what verses the women liked.

Day Two Study

- Read paragraph and "Focus on the Meaning." Ask Qs6-7.

- Read the definitions of words. Ask Qs8-9, including "Scriptural Insight."

- Read Ephesians 5:1-2, 22-25. Qs10-11 and "Scriptural Insight."

- Q12.

- Q13. Break up into groups of 3-4 to discuss. Consider pairing those with similar life circumstances together (married / single or widowed). Share some of the insights with the whole group.

Day Three Study

- Read Colossians 3:22-4:1. Qs14-16 and "Focus on the Meaning."

- Q17.

- Q18. Read 1 Peter 2:21-23; 3:1-6. Avoid rabbit trails. Focus on the heart choices.

- Read Acts 5:29. Qs19-20.

- Q21 and "Think About It."

- Skip Q22. Ask Q23.

Day Four Study

- Q24. Skip Q25.

- Q26. Discuss if someone has brought up something related to this lesson they have seen on the internet.

- Discuss the podcast topic using the listener guide. Ask questions based on your own insights and understanding.

- Read together the italicized paragraph at the end.

- Prayer time.

Recommendation: Listen to a worship song such as "Build Me Life" or "Lord, I Need You."

LESSON 10: MAKING A DIFFERENCE

Choose ahead of time which verses from the questions the group will read aloud as you proceed through the discussion. My recommendations are below.

Start with prayer.

Day One Study

- Read Colossians 4:2-18. Ask Qs1-2—quick answers. Skip Qs3-4. Ask Q5 to see what verses the women liked.

Day Two Study

- Ask Q6. Read "Focus on the Meaning." Discuss the second sentence.
- Qs7-9.
- Q10. Read the 1 Thessalonians and 1 Peter verses. Read "From the Greek."
- Qs11-13 and "Focus on the Meaning."
- Qs14-15.
- Q16. Break up into groups of 2 to practice.
- Q17 is personal.
- Discuss the podcast at this point since it fits with this part of the lesson. Ask what grabbed their attention. Talk about praying for and loving the unbelievers around them.

Day Three Study

- Q18. Let individuals take each person and read the verses in Colossians that apply.
- Qs19-20 and "Scriptural Insight."
- Q21.
- Read "What happened to the Colossian church?"

Day Four Study

- Q22.
- Q24 if you have anything to evaluate.
- Prayer time.

Recommendation: Listen to a worship song such as "Build My Life."

LESSON 11: FORGIVENESS AND RECONCILIATION

Choose ahead of time which verses from the questions the group will read aloud as you proceed through the discussion. My recommendations are below.

Start with prayer. You can start with asking if anyone has been wronged and how hard it is to get over it.

Day One Study

- Read Philemon 1-23. Ask Qs1, 3-4—quick answers. Skip Q2. Ask Q5 to see what verses the women liked.

Day Two Study

- Qs6-7.

- Give answer to Q8. Read "Historical Insight."

- Qs9-10. Read Colossians 4:9.

- Qs11-14.

Day Three Study

- Qs15-16. Skip "Think About It."

- Q17. Read Philemon 11 and "From the Greek."

- Qs18-19 and "Historical Insight."

- Q20.

- Have a sharing time at the end of Lesson 11 when they can share their passage and what the Lord taught them through it.

- Discuss the podcast at this point since it fits with this part of the lesson. Ask what grabbed their attention. Highlight what you think they need to discuss.

Day Four Study

- Q21.

- Read together the italicized paragraph at the end of the podcast on page 141.

- Prayer time.

Recommendation: Listen to a worship song such as "Lord, I Need You."

Sources

1. A. T. Robertson, *Word Pictures of the New Testament*
2. *Dr. Tom Constable's Notes on Colossians 2020 Edition*
3. Kay Arthur, *Lord, Is It Warfare?*
4. *NIV Study Bible*
5. *The Bible Knowledge Commentary (New Testament),* Walvoord and Zuck
6. *The Ryrie Study Bible*
7. Vickie Kraft quote from her Colossians teaching
8. *The Woman's Study Bible*
9. *Dr. Tom Constable's Notes on Philemon 2019 Edition*